THE MESSIAH COMES TO ISRAEL

Will a Major Bible Prophecy
Soon Be Fulfilled in Israel?

GERALD ROWLANDS

Author's Note: Whenever the word LORD appears in all uppercase letters in the English Bible, it is a translation of Yaweh (or Jehovah) the name of God, which is never used orally or in written form by Jewish people out of respect for the "unpronounceable name." However, I have used it sparingly to clearly differentiate between the God of Israel and Allah. I trust that Jewish readers will understand that no disrespect is intended of G-d or of Jewish tradition.

Please note that Destiny Image Europe's publishing style capitalizes certain pronouns in Scripture that refer to the Father, Son, and Holy Spirit, and may differ from some Bible publishers' styles. Take note that the name satan and related names are not capitalized. We choose not to acknowledge him, even to the point of violating grammatical rules.

DESTINY IMAGE™ EUROPE srl
Via Maiella, 1
66020 San Giovanni Teatino (Ch) – Italy

"Changing the world, one book at a time."

This book and all other Destiny Image™ Europe books are available at Christian bookstores and distributors worldwide.

To order products, or for any other correspondence:

DESTINY IMAGE™ EUROPE srl
Via Acquacorrente, 6
65123 - Pescara - Italy
Tel. +39 085 4716623 - Fax: +39 085 9431270
E-mail: info@eurodestinyimage.com
Or reach us on the Internet: www.eurodestinyimage.com

ISBN: 978-88-89127-99-5
For Worldwide Distribution, Printed in the U.S.A.
1 2 3 4 5 6 7 8 / 14 13 12 11 10

ENDORSEMENTS

There are so many excellent and important points and revelations in this book by Gerald Rowlands that I am happy to write a few words of endorsement.

Many of his points throw new light on the oh-so-important subject of the believer's attitude toward Israel, the great outpouring of God's Spirit soon to come upon the house of Israel, and the amazing military victories God is set to give Israel over all her enemies.

May this book be read with a truly open heart by many believers throughout the world, causing them to think again about their own personal response to God's miracle—Israel!

Jan Willem van der Hoeven
Director, International Christian Zionist Center

Gerald Rowlands has written an important book that every Christian needs to read. He writes with the sharp eyes of a watchman and the tender heart of a shepherd. His insights are critical reading for every serious believer who wants to understand God's prophetic plan for the days ahead.

Dr. Richard Booker
Author of *The Miracle of the Scarlet Thread,*
and various other books about Israel

TABLE OF CONTENTS

FOREWORDS

Gerald Rowlands's book, *The Messiah Comes to Israel,* tackles the subject of the future in a brilliant way. As a leading international Bible scholar and church planter, I believe his book should be required reading for every sincere seeker of truth concerning the future. His clear and logical presentation, based on a lifetime of study and analysis, carefully pieces together prophetic Scriptures in an original way. The resultant book brings comfort and blessing out of a subject that can be worrisome, if not downright frightening, for the average person.

Gerald Rowlands reveals the covenant-keeping character of the all-knowing, all-loving Father God in Heaven who not only knows the past and the present but the future as well. Instead of being a scary book, it is one through which the reader can "see" through. *The Messiah Comes to Israel* reveals a kind, merciful, and covenant-honoring Abba who is above all keen to reveal His plan for Israel and, of course, for all of humankind. After all, Israel is God's prophetic time piece, is it not?

Although Gerald has launched out into an ocean of rough waters where private interpretation of end-time events and wide-eyed date-setting down through the centuries has brought strong division among theologians, *The Messiah Comes To Israel,* thankfully does not fall into this trap.

As a student of the Bible and as a writer, I am sincerely grateful that Gerald has boldly penned for us the courage of his convictions. Yes, he has taken strong positions. Yet each time they are backed up with a panorama of scriptural quotes that lay a sure foundation for the prophetic future. Such authoritative conclusions are not often found in literature. But, by his own admission, he is still open to "course correction" and to "progressive revelation" by the Spirit of Truth. I like that approach.

I have always admired Gerald Rowlands as a dynamic Bible teacher; now my hat is off to him as an author who presents an interesting flow of information that clearly shows what is going to happen in the future—yet he has not painted himself into a doctrinal corner. As one of those who live in Jerusalem, the epicenter for the future for Jews, Arabs, and the international community alike, you have done us all a great service…thanks.

Dr. Jay Rawlings,
CEO Jerusalem Vistas/Israel Vision
www.israelvision.tv

The Messiah Comes to Israel contains a strategically essential message for the Church and Israel today. Gerald Rowlands does not give us another "end-times theory," but rather a clear reading of biblical prophecy regarding the very days in which we live! Most of us have inherited an eschatological viewpoint from a denomination, or developed one in keeping with our own spiritual DNA. We usually choose our particular view from a list of three or four scenarios held by theologians to be the only choices possible. All of those points of view have missing pieces. For the first time, Rowlands fills in some of those glaring missing pieces, and—like placing those last few puzzle pieces—brings a gratifying sense of wonder as a more complete picture comes into view. Gerald Rowlands gives not another choice, but a better view—there is something *more* that makes better sense of what we knew.

Some of us, spoiled for choice or weary of fruitless controversy, have wrongly opted out of the discussion. Here is a clear reading of Scripture that—rather than further clouding the issue—brings us to an "Aha!" moment as another puzzle piece falls suitably into place. I've been wrestling with the issues of Israel and the prophetic Word for over 30 years and have been waiting all this time for what

Gerald Rowlands brings to the table. In his own words, "I must have read Zechariah 12 dozens of times over the years before the full implications of this amazing chapter became clear."

This book presents answers to many profound questions such as: How and when does Israel experience revival? Does Israel meet her Messiah only to move effortlessly into the Messianic Age, or will she participate powerfully with the Church in a final advance of the Kingdom of God? Are *Gog and Magog* and *Armageddon* the only remaining wars predicted in the Bible, or is there another?

The Messiah Comes to Israel is a must-read for everyone with a heart to *pray for the peace of Jerusalem.* Psalm 122:6 speaks of being involved with the Lord's redemptive strategy for Jerusalem and the nations, of inquiring of the Lord about the progress—wholeness or completeness—of Jerusalem, and the advance of the Kingdom worldwide.

The final battle for Jerusalem belongs to this generation. Events in the Middle East are unfolding at a dizzying pace, and Christians cannot afford to watch passively from the sidelines. If we are to effectively engage in God's strategies for Israel, Islam, and the world, we need to take hold of them in prayer. Reverend Gerald Rowlands brings 50 years of teaching and ministry to bear in this book. It is an urgent apostolic message for the whole church that will empower our prayer and sharpen our prophetic perspective.

Rev. Joel Baker
Nambour Baptist Church
Queensland, Australia
(Note: Reverend Baker earned a Bachelor's degree in
Jewish Studies from the University of Washington, 1979, and a
Master's degree in Jewish-Christian Relations in Jerusalem, 1982)

PREFACE

I must have read Zechariah 12 dozens of times over the years before the full implication of verse 10 flooded my consciousness. The earlier verses of this amazing chapter predict a savage end-times attack upon Israel by all her nearest neighbors. Their ultimate aim is obviously to totally conquer and eradicate the nation of Israel. It appears that in the natural, this ambition is entirely capable of fulfillment unless some fundamental changes begin to happen in Israel.

The first indication of these changes occurs in Zechariah 12:4 when God says "...and I will open My eyes and regard with favor the house of Judah" (AMP).

A new season of divine favor will be launched over Israel. When all the nations on earth unite together against Israel (see Zech. 12:3), God will intentionally and powerfully stand with Israel and will release a fresh portion of His favor over the nation.

The second observable change will happen in the hearts of the leadership of Israel. The prophet declares in Zechariah 12:5 (AMP):

And the chiefs of Judah shall say in their hearts, the inhabitants of Jerusalem are our strength in the Lord of hosts, their God.

The Israeli government, with considerable good reason, has become confident about the ability of their remarkable defense force's ability to defend Israel from the wrath of her enemies. The Israeli Defense Force (IDF) has frequently demonstrated its amazing ability to snatch victory from the jaws of defeat. They have convincingly won numerous wars even when attacked by overwhelming armies of several nations combined in an effort to destroy Israel. But Zechariah indicates that under the ultimate threat staged by an alliance of nearby nations, the leaders of Israel will recognize their apparent vulnerability. Their confidence will then be transferred to the LORD of Hosts, the Holy One of Israel who is called the Commander of Heaven's armies. According to Zechariah 12, the Israeli Defense Force will be endued with supernatural strength and ability. The Israeli forces will become like a fiery torch in a field of dry grain, and they will devour all the enemy armies around them.

> *In that day will I make the chiefs of Judah like a big, blazing pot among [sticks of] wood and like a flaming torch among sheaves [of grain], and they shall devour all the peoples round about, on the right hand and on the left; and they of Jerusalem shall yet again dwell and sit securely in their own place, in Jerusalem* (Zechariah 12:6 AMP).

In the verses 8 and 9, the prophet vividly and succinctly describes the astounding victory that God will achieve on behalf of Israel:

> *In that day will the Lord guard and defend the inhabitants of Jerusalem, and he who is [spiritually] feeble and stumbles among them in that day [of persecution] shall become [strong and noble] like David; and the house of David [shall maintain its supremacy] like God, like the Angel of the Lord Who is before them. And it shall be in that day that I will make it My aim to destroy all the nations that come against Jerusalem* (Zechariah 12:8-9 AMP).

This amazing victory will be sensational, attracting worldwide attention and causing all humanity to recognize that Israel has been singly blessed with a direct intervention from her God. But what follows the victory is even more remarkable, for the source of the victory is found to be in the person of the "Angel of the Lord" who is none other than the Messiah of Israel. The Messiah will then reveal His true identity not only as the authentic Messiah, but also as the One who was once pierced in Jerusalem.

This already amazing sequence of events will become even more astounding as the whole nation of Israel, family by family, secular, political, and religious, enters a period of deep mourning such as has not been witnessed in Israel since the death of good King Josiah after the battle of Hadad Rimmon. The whole nation will be involved in a face-to-face meeting with their living God as they gaze upon Him with wonder and awe. They will also recognize that it was in fact God Himself who was pierced in the person of Yeshua, manifest as the Lamb of God. This awesome revelation propels Israel into a people with living faith in their newly discovered Messiah. It will be the beginning of a spiritual process by which Israel will truly become the holy nation that God has always desired them to become.

> *"Now if you will obey Me and keep My covenant, you will be My own special treasure from among all the nations on earth; for all the earth belongs to Me. And you will be My kingdom of priests, My holy nation." This is the message you must give to the people of Israel* (Exodus 19:5-6).

This tremendous outpouring of the Holy Spirit will not only come upon the Jews, the descendants of Abraham, it will also envelop the "inhabitants of Jerusalem" where not only Jews live, but also Christians and Muslims. All will be part of this glorious event and may emerge from it with the potential of becoming a great Messianic army representing the One New Man of whom Paul spoke (see Eph. 2:15) which is neither Jew nor Gentile but a combination of both.

The war that precedes this phenomenal transformation looks inevitable at this present time. In fact, it is already being waged to a small degree through the efforts of Hamas, the Sunni Muslim Palestinian extremist group based in Gaza, and Hezbollah, the Lebanese Islamic terrorist group, trained and equipped by Iran. The current president of Iran, Mahmoud Ahmadinejad, has frequently stated his determined intention to destroy the Jewish State of Israel[1] and is feverishly working to perfect his weapons of mass destruction (WMD).[2]

When this current threat becomes reality, God will have to intervene to keep Israel from being "wiped off the map" (see Ps. 83:4). If Israel is destroyed, many biblical predictions of God's favor and protection would be proved vain and worthless. But that will certainly not happen. When the predicted war of Zechariah 12, Psalm 83, and

Joel 3 is finally launched, the relevant Scriptures will be fulfilled in meticulous detail including the revelation of the Messiah to Israel.

This is the possibility I investigate in this book. I invite you to join me on an examination of the Scriptures concerning this predicted event.

I encourage an investigation from a Berean perspective (see Acts 17:11) into the possibility that Zechariah 12, and in particular the 10th verse, predicts an amazing supernatural Israeli victory followed by the literal appearance of the Messiah to Israel, and the resultant spiritual transformation of the nation.

Endnotes

1. Ezra HaLevi, "Iran Threatens to Destroy Israel"; http://www.israelnationalnews.com/News/News.aspx/101999; accessed December 19, 2009. "Ahmadinejad predicts Isarel will be swept away by Palestinians;" http://www.haaretz.com/hasen/spages/982998.html; accessed January 16, 2010.

2. Scott Peterson, *Christian Science Monitor*, 12/10/09; http://www.csmonitor.com/World/Middle-East/2009/1216/Iran-missile-test-follows-sanctions-talk-from-West; accessed December 19, 2009. Osama Bin Laden's Jihad and text of Fatwahs and Declaration of War; http://www.mideastweb.org/osamabinladen1.htm; accessed January 16, 2010.

Chapter One

ISRAEL'S FUTURE BECOMES HER PRESENT

Is one of the most amazing prophecies in the Bible about to be imminently fulfilled? Will Israel soon gaze on the face of her Messiah? Is it possible that this will happen in the very near future? How and when will it possibly happen?

These are the burning questions we will investigate together. According to the prophet Zechariah, and in the light of current events, this prediction may happen very soon:

- The determined threats of annihilation have already been issued.
- Israel's vicious and hostile enemies sit waiting on her borders.
- The stage, as described by Zechariah, is already in place.
- The battle appears almost ready to be launched.

When will this whole scenario be fulfilled in detail?

Throughout history many nations have sought to divide God's land, and today, once again, this has become an important issue among the world's nations. Many nations are saying that the division of the present land of Israel is absolutely imperative to procure peace in the Middle East. Almost every nation on earth, except Israel, is willing to divide God's land. The Muslim nations are the most vocal and insistent, but many other nations empathize with these countries and are urging the United Nations to once again divide the land of Israel. Many influential and powerful countries in the non-Islamic world are also using their political influence to force the division of Israel.[1] Little do they realize or understand the price they will eventually have to pay for their treacherous actions.

One of the most thrilling predictions in the Bible may take place in the very near future—the moment when the Messiah, after winning an astonishing victory for Israel, will reveal Himself to the whole nation. This amazing appearance is predicted by the prophet Zechariah, a passage which seems to be overlooked by most Bible students. Many Christian commentators seem to assign all of God's glorious promises for Israel to the Millennium, but I believe that many of them are going to be fulfilled before the Rapture, the Second Coming, or the Millennium. I am anticipating an era very soon when God will reveal His mercy, faithfulness, and glory to the whole world through His actions on behalf of the nation of Israel. The glorious predicted future of Israel will become a present miraculous reality!

> *And I will pour on the house of David **and on the inhabitants of Jerusalem** the Spirit of grace and supplication; **then they will look on Me whom they pierced**. Yes, they will mourn for Him as one mourns for his only son, and grieve for Him as one grieves for a firstborn* (Zechariah 12:10 NKJV).

This appearance will closely follow the amazing climax of a war launched upon Israel by all her closest neighbors. Such a war has already been launched through terrorist groups with the support of Iran, consistently raining rockets and missiles upon Israel.[2] There is bitter hatred in the hearts of militant Islamist extremists who are fanatically determined to annihilate Israel. This terrorist activity will certainly explode into a major attack on Israel that will threaten the very existence of the Jewish State. The attack will invite the personal intervention of God and the Angel of the Lord to rescue and deliver Israel.

I believe that as inevitable as this war is, so also is the certainty of God's intervention. And according to Zechariah, the revelation of the Messiah to Israel will be just as certain. For when Israel looks around in astonishment to see who rescued and delivered them, they will look upon Him, the Messiah of Israel. They will recognize Him and say, "Blessed are YOU who come in the name of the Lord." The nation will then begin to be transformed.

Even the most casual reader of the Bible must realize that God has a sovereign and unique plan for Israel and Jerusalem. The Bible is filled with God's plan and promises for Israel from Genesis to Revelation. Unfortunately, many readers focus either on ancient history or the dim, distant, seemingly ethereal future beyond the horizon. Events predicted for Israel "tomorrow," are actually being fulfilled today. The God of the Bible is not an ancient, antiquated being who lived 6,000 years ago. He is the God of this present hour and is working out His plans and purposes for the nations *now!* I propose that in the very near future God is going to fulfill some of the most amazing predictions in the Bible. This is not merely an interesting subject to study—they are amazing events to prepare for. Our theology and perceptions of end-time events must change to accommodate these amazing occurrences.

STUDY OF LAST THINGS AND END TIMES

Eschatology, the study of last things and End Times, is not an exact science. There are many different theories about what will happen when, and none can be actually proven. I encourage you to hold your particular views and perspectives carefully and consider what I am suggesting. What I will share here is not set in concrete in my own mind. I earnestly search the Scriptures and wait on the Lord for more light and understanding. However, what I am finding resonates well with my personal convictions and concerns for Israel as well as my own understanding of Scripture. I humbly invite you to join me in this journey of investigation.

Most Christian commentators and writers, when writing about end-time events, usually tread a very familiar and well-worn path. The material they cover most often falls into a predictable sequence of the same subjects. I have chosen to present some brief comments and descriptions that are typical of the positions and views of most evangelical churches that have an end-time theology. Many of these people vaguely believe in the "Last Days" and the Second Coming of Christ. However, very few recognize the specific prophetic role of Israel and how God's plan for Israel and the nations may soon eventuate. Nor do they realize how close we may currently be to these amazing events. Sadly, many people also subscribe to a view commonly known as Replacement Theology. This view teaches that the Church has permanently replaced Israel as the instrument through which God will fulfill His prophetic plan and eternal purpose. For them, the many promises made to Israel in the Bible (especially the Kingdom promises) are fulfilled in the Christian Church, in a nonliteral way.

The prophecies in Scripture concerning the blessing and restoration of Israel to the Land of Promise and the consequent glory are "spiritualized" into promises of God's blessing for the Church. Sadly, the prophecies of condemnation and judgment, according to this view, still remain for national Israel. The majority of such people basically believe that the next prophetic event to be fulfilled will be the pretribulation rapture of the Church and the ensuing suffering of a further holocaust for Israel in the Great Tribulation.

However, we are going to look closely at the possibility that there is yet another great and very important event to happen before any of these other prophecies are fulfilled.

The general trend and sequence of events according to the commonly held view is usually as follows.

1. THE RAPTURE OF THE CHURCH

In the Rapture of the Church perception of End Times, the Church is caught up to meet Jesus in the clouds and return with Him to Heaven to celebrate the Marriage Supper of the Lamb. While they are celebrating, Israel will be experiencing and enduring the greatest period of tribulation in their whole existence. I personally have great difficulty imagining a great scene of superlative rejoicing in Heaven with the Messiah, while at the same time Israel is experiencing her greatest time of suffering on earth. I do not dispute that Israel will be present during the Great Tribulation but I do believe that she will experience great victories and triumphs during that time as she rejoices together with the innumerable company in the efficacy of the Lamb of God.

And crying out with a loud voice, saying, "Salvation belongs to our God who sits on the throne, and to the Lamb!" (Revelation 7:10 NKJV)

2. THE GOG AND MAGOG WAR (EZEKIEL 38 AND 39)

In this prophecy about the Gog and Magog war, Russia and several Muslim nations launch a joint attack on Israel described in Ezekiel 38:11-12 (NKJV):

You will say, 'I will go up against a land of unwalled villages; I will go to a peaceful people, who dwell safely, all of them dwelling without walls, and having neither bars nor gates'—to take plunder and to take booty, to stretch out your hand against the waste places that are again inhabited, and against a people gathered from the nations, who have acquired livestock and goods, who dwell in the midst of the land.

Once again the judgment of God will come upon enemy armies seeking to invade and conquer Israel.

"And it will come to pass at the same time, when Gog comes against the land of Israel," says the Lord GOD, "that My fury will show in My face. For in My jealousy and in the fire of My wrath I have spoken: 'Surely in that day there shall be a great earthquake in the land of Israel' "(Ezekiel 38:18-19 NKJV).

3. THE GREAT TRIBULATION

The Great Tribulation will be a relatively short but very intense period of great distress and suffering at the end of time. The popular view is that it will last for seven years (two periods of three and one half years). The phrase, Great Tribulation, is found only once in the Bible (see Rev. 7:14). The great tribulation is said to fulfill Daniel's prophecies (see Dan. 7–12). It will be a time of evil involving a false Christ and other false prophets (see Mark 13:22) when natural disasters will occur throughout the world. It will be a period of trouble, confusion, and tribulation such as the world has never previously experienced.

4. THE ANTI-CHRIST'S REIGN

The anti-Christ is a false prophet and an evil character who will set himself up in place of and against the true Christ and the people of God during the great tribulation. It refers to one who stands in the place of and in opposition to all that Jesus Christ represents (see 1 John 2:18,22; 4:3; 2 John 7). John wrote that several anti-Christs existed already in his day—false teachers—who denied the deity and the atoning death and resurrection of Christ.

5. THE BATTLE OF ARMAGEDDON

The Battle of Armageddon is said to take place on the mountain of Megiddo and will be the site of the great final battle of this age in which God intervenes to destroy the armies of satan and to cast satan into the bottomless pit (see Rev. 16:16; 20:1-3,7-10). *Armageddon* is the Greek word for this area, which was the scene of many ancient historic battles. Because of this history, Megiddo became a symbol of the final conflict between God and the forces of evil. According to the Book of Revelation, at Armageddon "the cup of the wine of the fierceness of His [God's] wrath" (Rev. 16:19 NKJV) will be poured out, and the forces of evil will be overthrown and destroyed.

6. THE SECOND COMING OF CHRIST TO EARTH

The Second Coming of Christ is Christ's future return to the earth accompanied by His saints at the end of the present age. The apostle John says,

> *Behold, He is coming with clouds, and every eye will see Him, even they who pierced Him. And all the tribes of the earth will mourn because of Him. Even so, Amen* (Revelation 1:7 NKJV).

This is seen to be the occasion when all the saints of Christ who were raptured before the Great Tribulation and have attended the Marriage Supper of the lamb will accompany Jesus back to earth. The phrase "Second Coming" does not occur anywhere in the New Testament. However, many passages, speak of His return to earth. Immediately before Jesus ascended to Heaven, the Bible tells us,

Now when He had spoken these things, while they watched, He was taken up, and a cloud received Him out of their sight. And while they looked steadfastly toward heaven as He went up, behold, two men stood by them in white apparel, who also said, "Men of Galilee, why do you stand gazing up into heaven? This same Jesus, who was taken up from you into heaven, will so come in like manner as you saw Him go into heaven" (Acts 1:9-11 NKJV).

The New Testament refers to this event over 300 times. Jesus said concerning His return that only the Father knew the exact time when it would happen. However, most scholars say it will occur at the end of the Tribulation. The return of the Lord should be a matter of constant expectation and anticipation. As Jesus came the first time, in the "fullness of time" (see Gal. 4:4), so will the Second Coming be. The believer's task is not to try to determine the *time* of the Second Coming but to spiritually *prepare* for it. We should share the Kingdom message diligently and passionately until He returns (see Matt. 24:14).

7. THE MILLENNIAL REIGN OF CHRIST (REVELATION 20)

The Millennial reign of Christ is the thousand-year period mentioned in connection with the description of Christ's coming to reign with His saints over the earth (see Rev. 19:11-16; 20:1-9). Many Old Testament passages refer to the Millennium (see Isa. 11:4; Jer. 3:17; Zech. 14:9 etc). The one thousand years is *not* the full period of Christ's reign over the earth. The prophet Daniel says of Messiah:

...His kingdom is an everlasting kingdom, and His dominion is from generation to generation (Daniel 4:3 NKJV).

The emphasis of John on the thousand-year period is that satan will be bound for that time in the bottomless pit. He will not deceive the nations until his short period of release at the end of the Millennium (see Rev. 20:3,7-8). After one thousand years, satan will be loosed for a brief period, but his plans will be finally thwarted. The saints of God will be resurrected. They will rule with Christ and will be priests of God and Christ (see Rev. 5:10; 20:4). The unbelieving dead will wait for the second resurrection (see Rev. 20:5). After the thousand years, satan will be released and will resume his work of deceit (see Rev. 20:7-8).

ANOTHER VIEW

I propose that there is an amazing and supernatural event which will precede all of these events. It is like the missing piece of a giant jigsaw puzzle entitled "the mystery of the ends of the age." I have always felt that the reason why God would regather the tribes of Israel in the last days and bring them back to their Promised Land was to bless, exalt, and promote them before the eyes of the world. I cannot conceive that He would lure them all back to have them go through another fearful holocaust and be severely mauled and mutilated there. God has made so many glorious predictions concerning Israel that have not yet been fulfilled. Surely He would not wait until the Millennium to accomplish all of these great promises? He obviously wants to display before the world what a nation under His covenantal blessing looks like. This example will be a tremendous challenge to the nations to surrender to the rule of Messiah and His Kingdom. We who are His watchmen must pray to that end.

> *I have set watchmen on your walls, O Jerusalem; they shall never hold their peace day or night. You who make mention of the LORD, do not keep silent, and give Him no rest till **He establishes and till He makes Jerusalem a praise in the earth*** (Isaiah 62:6-7 NKJV).

In my proposal I am certainly not wishing to ignore, dispute, or deny the other prophetic events. Rather, I am stating that another great end-time prophecy will be fulfilled before any of these other events transpire. It is an event that will surely change our perspective about the traditional prophetic end-time calendar. Then it will introduce an era in which Israel will enjoy the favor of God and the fulfillment of so many wonderful statements and promises that God has made concerning Israel and Jerusalem.

The fulfillment of what Zechariah 12:10 predicts will transform Israel into a Messianic nation from which a symbolic army of evangelists will come forth (see Rev. 7:4-8). They, together with an innumerable company of men and women from every people group on earth, will proclaim the salvation and Kingdom of our God.

> *After these things I looked, and behold, a great multitude which no one could number, of all nations, tribes, peoples, and tongues, standing before the throne and before the Lamb, clothed with white robes, with palm branches in their hands, and crying out with a loud voice, saying, "Salvation belongs to our God who sits on the throne, and to the Lamb!" All the angels stood around the throne and the elders and the four living creatures, and fell on their faces before the throne and worshiped God, say-ing: "Amen! Blessing and glory and wisdom, Thanksgiving and honor and power and might, Be to our God forever and ever. Amen"* (Revelation 7:9-12 NKJV).

As mentioned previously, for many Christians, Bible prophecies have always seemed to refer to an ethereal dim and distant future too far away to be awaited with any degree of practical interest. The sub-ject of End Times and the study of prophetic events have often been treated as some kind of religious or superstitious gimmick. It is a line of teaching that is perceived as something of a detour from reality. Many younger believers have filed it in the "too difficult to under-stand basket" and left it to the older generation. But we are now living in the time period when these prophecies are clearly on the horizon. We are moving into the era when prophecies concerning the future are becoming present realities. Every believer needs to understand the proximity of the literal fulfillment of Bible predictions and live in the light and understanding of the times in which we now live.

Amidst all the confusion in our present world, perhaps nothing is more certain than the prospect of a gigantic war upon Israel launched by her surrounding Muslim neighbors. It is also very clear that such a war will have profound and devastating effects worldwide. For many years I have said that the next great battle the world would face would not be between Communism and Western Democracy but between Judeo Christianity and militant Islam. Many political and military commentators can now clearly foresee such a war. What they cannot see is the amazing victory that will be won for Israel and the exciting spiritual transformation that will ensue following that war.

Zechariah 12 is obviously a prophetic event awaiting fulfillment. The first nine verses describe a war launched upon Israel by all neighboring countries. This is a war which is graphically described in several parts of the Bible and I believe will happen soon. The early stages of this battle are already being fought and threaten to continue and escalate. The battle will erupt again with far more devastating violence, and Israel's very existence will be seriously threatened. Zechariah 12:10 describes a particularly sensational happening when, following the great victory described in the preceding verses, God will pour out His Holy Spirit upon Israel and Jerusalem. The Holy Spirit will convey grace, prayers, and repentance to the entire nation after which God will reveal His true Messianic identity to Israel. This predicted war and the amazing aftermath looms large on our present horizon. The stage is already set. The battle will soon be enjoined again. If this war is inevitable, the predicted revelation of Messiah to the Jewish nation is also inevitable.

What will be the ongoing result of this astonishing event? When is it likely to happen? What will the world look like in the wake of this prophetic fulfillment? Only the Bible holds the answers to these vital questions. This book presents some possibilities.

FOUR THINGS ARE CERTAIN

1. Islam will never relinquish its avowed determination to conquer, possess, and dominate Israel and Jerusalem.
2. God will never allow this to happen.
3. The victory that God grants Israel will precede a great outpouring of His Spirit of grace, prayers, and repentance upon Israel and Jerusalem and a glorious revelation of the true identity of the Messiah (see Zech 12:10).
4. The Messiah will reveal His true Jewish identity to Israel, and they will receive Him as the One who comes in the name of the LORD.

One challenging question now confronts us. When are these amazing events likely to happen, and does their fulfillment await us in the very near future?

A MASSIVE TIME BOMB

A devastating war sits like a massive time bomb waiting to explode upon Israel. The indications are all too clear. The current leader of Iran, in my opinion a fanatic, has declared his intention to the whole world. He is presently waging the earliest stages of this war through well-known terrorist groups in Gaza and Lebanon—Hamas and Hezbollah. The escalation of this war is inevitable. Though few have yet recognized the fact, the Bible actually predicts this war in graphic detail. I believe the fulfillment of those predictions will happen in the very near future. Built into one of those prophecies is a predicted appearance of the Messiah that will cause a sensational transformation in Israel the effects of which will reverberate around the world.

The most important question may be, "When will it all happen?"

For some years now, Israel has been living under the serious threat and threshold of a possible nuclear war and complete annihilation. The threats have been consistently made by the president of Iran and the religious Mullahs who support him. President Ahmadinejad is capable of anything; a very dangerous person whose threats need to be seriously considered. He is a Haman/Hitler-type tyrant who must not be underestimated. He has spent billions of dollars of his nation's national budget to produce weapons that include nuclear and chemical warheads.[3] He has also been supplied with long-range, high-tech missiles from various other nations including Russia that are capable of reaching targets thousands of miles from Iran bearing highly destructive warheads.[4]

Ahmadinejad has already launched the early stages of this war under the auspices of his minions in Syria, Lebanon, Gaza, and Egypt. Thousands of highly trained terrorists—fanatics who have dedicated their lives to the cause of destroying Israel—have already launched several efforts to attack, invade, and destroy the structure of the Jewish State, but each attack so far has been defeated. Nevertheless, they continue to persuade themselves that their task is not an impossible one. They are constantly planning more effective attacks and have surreptitiously gained the support of numerous nations and organizations. The world in general and the church in particular need to realize that the threats against Israel are more than empty words. They are explicit, intentional, and extremely serious. Not only is Israel under constant intimidation, but the entire world will suffer fearful repercussions from such a war.

Interpreting this scenario through Islam's apocalyptic lens, militant Muslims believe that the hour is near for their messiah (Il Mahdi) to make his messianic appearance and to establish Islam as the world's leading religious and political power through a massive military victory over hated Israel and the despised West. As the Western coalition struggles and wavers about Iran's threats and missile tests, Islamic confidence grows that victory, not only over Israel but over the West as well, is not only possible, but close at hand. If the balance of power is not rectified soon, the free world will experience a violent storm overflowing the West as never before, with terrorism striking civilian targets worldwide.

The Bible's Clear Prediction

Few people have recognized the Bible's clear prediction about this battle. Even fewer are truly convinced that it will happen any time soon. Even though the Bible foretells it in precise detail and the present world situation confirms it, most people would rather ignore the possibility. Secularists of all shades have tried to prove that the Bible is outmoded, inaccurate, and unreliable. But they will soon see that Bible prophecy concerning the days in which we now live, is meticulously accurate and considerably detailed.

Hundreds of prophecies that occur in the Bible have already been fulfilled with amazing accuracy. These were mainly concerning the first coming of Christ to earth. However, there are yet many predictions to be fulfilled concerning the End Times of this age. Some of those prophecies refer to a war that will be launched upon Israel by her closest neighbors and backed by several other nations. We will look into some of these prophecies in Psalm 83, Joel 3, Zechariah 12, and elsewhere in God's Word. Not only does the Bible predict an amazing, startling, supernatural victory for Israel, it also predicts the greatest event that has happened to Israel since the exodus from Egypt. It will be the spiritual re-birth and transformation of Israel as a precursor to a worldwide harvest from all nations into the Kingdom of God.

In some respects, Bible prophecy is somewhat like a giant jigsaw puzzle. The many pieces of the puzzle are scattered throughout the Bible from Genesis to Revelation and need to be sorted out and positioned in their correct places before the whole picture emerges. These pieces can be found in Daniel, Isaiah, Zechariah, Matthew, Mark, Luke, Revelation, and in many other parts of the Bible. I would like to put together some of those pieces that relate to the next great prophecy that awaits fulfillment, namely the battle for Jerusalem waged by her surrounding neighbors.

THE BATTLE FOR JERUSALEM

Many Christians and Bible commentators believe the next war will be the one forecast in Ezekiel 38 and 39, but there many pieces in that particular prophecy that do not fit the template. I have always thought that regarding the traditional picture of End Times, there was a huge gap. This gap is the fulfillment of many promises of greatness and splendor to Israel. Such promises are quite numerous, and I find it extremely difficult to assign the fulfillment of them all to the Millennium as so many commentators do. I believe that the missing piece of Bible prophecy is the private appearance of Messiah to His Jewish brethren following the battle for Jerusalem waged by its closest neighbors.

Israel has been consistently degraded, dishonored, and ridiculed throughout history, and the nations have so often sarcastically cried out, "Where is your God?" Surely God's honor and faithfulness must be displayed before the eyes of those same nations and not solely in some idyllic Millennium future paradise.

Ezekiel vividly sums up God's promised intentions for Israel in the last days.

The LORD said, "None of the surrounding nations that treated Israel with scorn will ever again be like thorns and briers to hurt Israel. And they will know that I am the Sovereign LORD." The Sovereign LORD said, "I will bring back the people of Israel from the nations where I scattered them, and all the nations will know that I am holy. The people of Israel will live in their own land, the land that I gave to my servant Jacob. They will live there in safety. They will build houses and plant vineyards. I will punish all their neighbors who treated them with scorn, and Israel will be secure. Then they will know that I am the LORD their God" (Ezekiel 28:24-26 GNT).

EZEKIEL FORETELLS GOD'S ACCOMPLISHMENTS FOR ISRAEL

1. None of Israel's surrounding neighbors will ever again treat Israel with scorn.
2. Those very nations will know and acknowledge that the God of the Bible is the one true God.
3. All nations on earth will recognize Jehovah as the Sovereign Lord of the universe.
4. The people of Israel will live in their own land.
5. They will live in safety, building houses and planting vineyards.
6. God will punish the nations who poured scorn on Israel.
7. They will all know that Jehovah God is supreme.

A MODERN-DAY HAMAN HAS ARISEN

The Book of Esther is coming to life again. And God is calling out to those who "have come to the Kingdom for such a time as this" to be watchmen on behalf of Jerusalem. The great drama was originally played out on the stage of Persia (modern Iran) when a psychopathic killer named Haman determined to annihilate all Jews throughout a vast kingdom. The thrilling story of how God intervened and saved the Jews through the intervention of a young Jewish girl named Esther is still celebrated to this day by Jewish people everywhere. How ironic that another tyrant has taken center stage in Iran and declared to the world his intention to annihilate the Jewish State and restore their land to Islamic rule.

Believers who recognize that Bible prophecy is accurate to the finest detail understand that history often repeats itself and that this will be the case with Iran. First, because a new potential destroyer has arisen breathing out fearsome threats against Jews. Second, because God will once again outwit the destroyer and obliterate him. Israel is about to be dramatically rescued once again, and the ultimate result will be even more sensational than was her deliverance from Egypt.

IRAN IS FRANTICALLY STOCKPILING NUCLEAR WARHEADS AND MISSILES[5]

Collaborating with Syria, Lebanon, Russia, North Korea, and China, Iran has been working for several years on a plan to wipe out the Jewish presence in "Palestine." Not only has Ahmadinejad made verbal threats of annihilation, he has also taken many concrete steps toward his objective by working to produce a nuclear arsenal at tremendous expense. Not even a madman would expend so much money, time and effort on a project he had no intention of fulfilling. The scenario is similar to what happened in Germany in the 1930s. Initially the world did not take Hitler seriously. Although he had laboriously made his plans widely known, no one took him seriously until he had invaded and devastated several European nations. By the time the world awoke to the dreadful reality that Hitler meant to carry out his plans, it was too late to save millions from tragedy and genocide.

ISLAMIC RESOLVE AND DETERMINATION

Some Islamic fanatics have a maniacal and fanatical dedication that defies the understanding of the non-Muslim world. The perpetrators of international terrorism are filled with a dark obsession with death. Christians may talk, preach, and sing about the impending Kingdom of God, but their dedication to its reality pales desperately compared to the dedication of some Islamic disciples. When most Christians speak of dying with Christ, they usually have a sentimental, idealistic euphoria coupled with a purely spiritual application. In complete contrast, when Muslims volunteer for martyrdom, they have a very real purpose in mind such as strapping a bomb around their waist and killing a group of innocent people. The extreme Islamist vision of world domination is not a fairytale. Advocates fully intend to gain complete superiority over all humanity; many are prepared to enthusiastically lay down their lives to attain it.

PROPHECY PREDICTS WAR OUTCOME

As mentioned previously, the war that will soon be launched by Israel's nearest neighbors will ultimately produce an amazing, supernatural victory for Israel. The Israel Defense Force, which has already gained deserved respect through victories against overwhelming odds, will gain a victory that will eclipse all previous victories. This time it will not be Israel's military skills and strategies that will win the day. It will be recognized by every nation on earth that this victory has been procured with direct supernatural divine assistance. The world will stand amazed in awe and wonder before the supernatural event in Israel.

THE MESSIANIC UNVEILING

Isaiah prophesied that God's servant (the Messiah) would bring Jacob back to Him and gather Israel to Him. He further declared that this task was too small for Messiah and that He would also be a Light to the Gentiles to bring salvation to the ends of the earth.

> *"And now the LORD says, who formed Me from the womb to be His Servant, to bring Jacob back to Him, so that Israel is gathered to Him (for I shall be glorious in the eyes of the LORD, and My God shall be My strength), indeed He says, 'It is too small a thing that You should be My Servant to raise up the tribes of Jacob, And to restore the preserved ones of Israel; I will also give You as a light to the Gentiles, that You should be My salvation to the ends of the earth'"* (Isaiah 49:5-6 NKJV).

Immediately after the victory has been won, the world will witness tremendous spiritual phenomena, when their Deliverer will reveal His true identity as the long-promised Messiah of Israel.

THE PRIESTLY, PROPHETIC, AND KINGLY NATION

The word *Messiah* comes from a Hebrew term meaning "anointed one." Its Greek translation is *Christos*, from which the English word *Christ* comes. There are three anointings in biblical tradition, the Priestly, Prophetic, and Kingly anointings. Jesus received all these anointings. Is Zechariah 12:10 prophetic of Israel's coronation?

Israel will become a truly Messianic nation when God pours upon her the anointing of the Holy Spirit and reveals His Messiah. A great army of reapers from the ranks of the house of David will combine with a multitude of Gentile believers to be the One New Man and reap the greatest harvest of all from a world that is experiencing great tribulation. The awe and reverence of God will be upon all the nations (see Rev. 7).

On several occasions, God has promised to pour out His Spirit upon Israel as a nation. These outpourings will happen in the Last Days. (See Ezekiel 37:13-14 and Ezekiel 39:29.)

Joel says, "it shall come to pass afterward" (Joel 2:28). After what? It will happen after the outpouring of the Spirit in Zechariah 12:10.

THE SPIRIT UPON ALL FLESH (JOEL 2:28)

*And it shall come to pass afterward that **I will pour out My Spirit on all flesh;** your sons and your daughters shall prophesy, your old men shall dream dreams, your young men shall see visions* (Joel 2:28 NKJV).

This particular promised outpouring was only partially fulfilled on the Day of Pentecost (see Acts 2). Although Peter quoted Joel's prophecy (see Joel 2:28-31) as an explanation for what was happening, the sun was not darkened on that day. Nor were there fires and pillars of smoke. It was obviously not the "great and awesome day of the Lord" that Joel had predicted. Several predicted aspects of that day were conspicuously absent. However, the Spirit will be poured out in His fullness when Zechariah 12:10 is fulfilled. This greatest of all outpourings will cause the nation of Israel to be mightily transformed and re-born in one day.

I believe that Zechariah 12:10 is the time of which Jesus spoke in Matthew 23:37-39 when Israel will say, "Blessed are You who comes in the name of the Lord."

> *O Jerusalem, Jerusalem, the one who kills the prophets and stones those who are sent to her! How often I wanted to gather your children together, as a hen gathers her chicks under her wings, but you were not willing! See! Your house is left to you desolate; for I say to you, you shall see Me no more till you say, "Blessed is He who comes in the name of the LORD!"*
> (Matthew 23:37-39 NKJV)

Jesus was specifically addressing Jerusalem and those who represented the ones who had rejected the prophets sent to her. He was addressing the Jewish leaders both political and religious. His inference was that Israel would not "recognize" Him until the day when they would loudly declare, "Blessed are You who comes in the name of the LORD."

A PERIOD OF PEACE AND PROSPERITY

The Bible is replete with wonderful promises regarding the supreme, ultimate glory of Jerusalem and Israel. The prophets frequently waxed lyrical about the splendors of Zion. Most Christian Bible commentators have assigned the fulfillment of these predictions to the Millennium. Could it be possible that the predictions will be fulfilled in the period immediately following the startling appearance and unveiling of Messiah to the house of David? Following is a brief timeline for reference.

1. Our present time period.
2. War on Israel. (Ps. 83, Zech. 12)
3. Messiah's unveiling to His Jewish audience.

4. Period of peace, prosperity, expansion.

5. Gog and Magog war. (Ezek. 38–39)

Ezekiel 38:10-12 speaks of Israel as a nation with sufficient "spoil" to warrant an attempted massive invasion to plunder that spoil.

Ezekiel also speaks of a people dwelling in peace and prosperity—that certainly does not represent the Jerusalem of today. Nobody can currently say that Israel is a peaceful and prosperous nation dwelling in safety and security. This prophecy relates to an Israel yet in the future. (Hopefully in the period following Israel's Zechariah12:10 anointing.)

We know that in the Book of Revelation where John spoke of the Millennium, he saw a glorious and magnificent city. (See Revelation 21:1-4.) However, it is equally clear that Messiah will come to the present city of Jerusalem and adorn it with His presence and glory. His radiant presence will dramatically transform Jerusalem into a visible measure of beauty and perfection!

And in Isaiah, I personally believe that the period to which Isaiah refers will be the dawning of this glorious new day for Israel and Jerusalem as foretold in Isaiah 60 and 61:

> *Arise, Jerusalem! Let your light shine for all to see. For the glory of the LORD rises to shine on you. Darkness as black as night covers all the nations of the earth, but the glory of the Lord rises and appears over you. All nations will come to your light; mighty kings will come to see your radiance* (Isaiah 60:1-3).

I believe that we are living in a frightening but glorious time. We are living in a day when many great tragedies will stalk the earth but ultimately it is a time when God is going to manifest His glory first through Israel and Jerusalem.

The Scriptures say that the "glory of the Lord will eventually cover the earth even as the waters cover the sea." We are moving rapidly toward a time when God will powerfully intervene in the affairs of humankind, when He will call time upon the confusion and destruction that man has brought upon himself. It will be a time when He will intervene, not in just some spiritual way but He will intervene visibly and manifestly to bring His Kingdom rule upon the earth.

ENDNOTES

1. *Financial Times*, "Israel's Revealing Fury Toward EU"; http://www.ft.com/cms/s/0/ba991878-e811-11de-8a02-00144feab49a.html?nclick_check=1; accessed December 19, 2009.

2. Haaretz Service, "Two Qassams Hit Israel in Second Gaza Rocket Attack this Week"; http://www.haaretz.com/hasen/spages/1135530.html; accessed December 19, 2009.

3. William J. Broad, Mark Mazzetti and David E. Sanger, "A Nuclear Debate—Is Iran Designing Warheads?" *New York Times*; http://www.nytimes.com/2009/09/29/world/middleeast/29nuke.html?_r=1; accessed December 19, 2009.

4. Charles Digges, "Russian Nuke Technicians Flood Iran for Final Push at Bushehr Reactor," Bellona, 3/9/02; http://www.bellona.org/english_import_area/international/russia/nuke_industry/co-operation/25570; accessed January 16, 2010. BBC News, "Russia Confirms Iran Missile Deal," 12/5/05; http://news.bbc.co.uk/2/hi/europe/4500878.stm; accessed January 16, 2010.

5. Iran Watch—Tracking Iran's Mass Destruction Weapon Capabilities; http://www.iranwatch.org/; accessed January 16, 2010. Eric Margolis, "Muslim Weapons of Mass Destruction," 3/9/09; http://www.ericmargolis.com/political_commentaries/muslim-weapons-of-mass-destruction.aspx; accessed January 16, 2010. CNN.com, "Iran test-fires long-range missiles," 9/28/09; http://www.cnn.com/2009/WORLD/meast/09/28/iran.missile.tests/index.html; accessed January 16, 2010.

Chapter Two

ISRAEL'S PENDING TRANSFORMATION: AN IMMINENT FULFILLMENT?

*Before going into labor, she gave birth; before her pains came,
she delivered a male child. Who ever heard of such a thing? Who
has ever seen such things? Is a country born in one day? Is a nation brought forth all at once? For as soon as Tziyon went into
labor, she brought forth her children* (Isaiah 66:7-8 CJB).

It is a popular belief among many Christians and Jews that the
Scripture in Isaiah 66 was fulfilled on May 14, 1948, in Tel Aviv
when David Ben Gurion, the first Prime Minister of Israel, declared the sovereignty of the new Jewish State. This is true in
many ways, for the Bible does certainly predict the re-gathering of
the Jews from the four corners of the earth to the land of their
forefathers. This migration, which had commenced slowly in the
late 1800s, gathered new momentum in 1948 following the war
that had been launched against the fledgling State by her angry
Arab neighbors.

Today, the modern State of Israel flourishes as the only democracy
in the Middle East and has achieved amazing success in re-settling
Jewish immigrants from all the nations of her Diaspora. Israel has
also successfully defended herself in several major wars when again
her immediate neighbors sought to destroy and annihilate the Jewish
State. In spite of every attempt to dislodge her, Israel with God's
help has remained in her place.

But is the present State of Israel truly *the* fulfillment of Isaiah 66:7-8? Or did God have a greater and higher purpose in mind when He inspired that scripture?

I believe that it should be clear to the unbiased mind that a secular state, however successful, was not God's highest ambition for Israel. He had declared in the earliest years of Israel's existence that Israel was to be a special and unique nation before Him in the earth. On numerous occasions, God predicted their remarkable future greatness. Unfortunately, most commentators including contemporary scholars have relegated the fulfillment of these predictions to the millennium because they could not perceive the fulfillment in any earlier prophetic era. Their view has often been influenced by the traditional "Rapture-Great Tribulation" view and a replacement type of theology that completely discards Israel from God's plans. However, the era immediately following the fulfillment of Zechariah 12:10 surely suggests the perfect opportunity for these glorious promises to be fulfilled.

THE PERFECTION OF BEAUTY

God calls Jerusalem the perfection of beauty—"Out of Zion, the perfection of beauty, God will shine forth" (Psalm 50:2 NKJV).

Perfection speaks of something far beyond excellence. It intimates something absolutely faultless and flawless. Even the most ardent lover of Jerusalem could not claim such for the present city. Is God going to await the Millennium before making it perfect? I think not. (Of course the New Jerusalem of the Millennium will be even more spectacular and glorious!)

When Elohim, the Creator of the universe, looked on what He had created in all its perfection (see Gen. 1), He declared that everything was "very good." What then might we anticipate when He declares something to be "the perfection of beauty?" In all its history, Jerusalem has been often greatly admired but never yet declared perfect. What the psalmist is describing is a vision of the future glorified city. In the period following Messiah's appearance to Israel, we will see a building up and beautifying of Jerusalem; but this "renovation" will not yet be the ultimate glorifying of Jerusalem that will finally happen in the eternal Kingdom.

Despite these and many other predictions of greatness that are being partially fulfilled in Israel even now, they are all eclipsed in the statement made in Exodus 19:6 in which God declares that Israel would become a holy nation and a kingdom of priests.

> *You have seen what I did to the Egyptians, and how I bore you on eagles' wings and brought you to Myself. Now therefore, if you will indeed obey My voice and keep My covenant, then you shall be a special treasure to Me above all people; for all the earth is Mine.* **And you shall be to Me a kingdom of priests and a holy nation These are the words which you shall speak to the children of Israel** *(Exodus 19:4-6 NKJV).*

God is Himself essentially holy. The word holy comes from a root word that means "to separate." Thus, it refers to God as exalted above all other things (see Isa. 6:1-3). Holiness refers to God's moral excellence, His supreme righteousness and perfection. Amazingly, He refers to a city, Jerusalem, that will one day reflect the same characteristics as Himself. There is an inherent beauty in the holiness of God and in everything He endows or dwells in. One day that beauty will adorn the city of Jerusalem.

Exodus 19:4-6 presents the solemn covenantal assuring prediction that one day Israel will be a holy nation and a kingdom of priests. Before that day, she will face many trials and eventually be brought to a place where, through the pressures she endures, she will completely surrender to God and His once-pierced Messiah. Is this the time of which Zechariah spoke?

Could it be the time that will immediately follow the local war on Israel and the outpouring of God's Spirit, a national time of mourning and repentance and the unveiling of Messiah's identity as the One who was pierced?

Isaiah gives some indication of the joy this day will occasion for Israel. The birthing of which he speaks will be a speedy one. The actual delivery will be swift and safe. The one who brings the pregnancy to its conclusion will not then close the womb and abort the child.

> *"Shall I bring to the time of birth, and not cause delivery?" says the LORD. "Shall I who cause delivery shut up the womb?" says your God. "Rejoice with Jerusalem, And be glad with her, all you who love her; Rejoice for joy with her, all you who mourn for her"* (Isaiah 66:9-10 NKJV).

WHO HAS HEARD SUCH A THING?

The miracle of Israel's ultimate transformation will be miraculous and inexpressible. Words will fail any attempt to describe the wonder, splendor and majesty when God finally glorifies His ancient covenant people, land, and city. An intrinsic aspect of that wondrous amazement will be the speed with which it will happen. The whole world will wonder, *how can a nation be so gloriously transformed in so short a time?* God says that, *"as soon as Zion was in labor she gave birth to her children."* Israel is certainly experiencing labor pains and contractions right now, but God has promised that the labor will not be too long—for suddenly Zion will give birth to her children. This will be great cause for rejoicing in Jerusalem among all those who have previously been in mourning for her.

Sadly for many "Christians," this amazing event will be all the more surprising because in their minds and theological interpretations, Israel has ceased to be a nation of interest to God. Such people choose to believe that God has finished with Israel and He has turned instead to the Gentiles. They have all manner of reasons why this is so, but the main reason cited is that Israel did not only reject the Messiah but actually killed Him.

Millions of other Christians may be taken by surprise because their belief system has not included a climax of the ages and the various phases by which this will come to pass. Although Christ is in their hearts by faith, they have not been renewed in the spirit of their minds to capture the thrilling fact that Jesus Christ is literally going to return to planet Earth in the near future. Nor have they searched the Scriptures thoroughly in order to determine all that this return will mean for Israel, the Church, and the world generally.

There are also many other Christians who do believe in the ultimate return of Christ in what has become known as the Rapture— when the Church will be evacuated from this earthly scene and all its problems. For the most part, these Christians believe that once the Church has been spirited away, the Great Tribulation will come upon the earth and Israel will be left alone to experience still another dreadful holocaust under the terror-filled reign of the anti-Christ and his empire. These particular Christians have given little thought to what God's specific plan is for the future of Israel.

There are also still many Christians who believe that the entire future plan of God relates to living eternally in Heaven, a planet millions of light years away from Earth. Even though some may now vaguely believe that the throne of Christ on Earth will be situated in Jerusalem, they have paid little attention as to what will be the particular role of Israel in the earthly kingdom and how this role may eventuate.

I personally believe that an intentional examination of Bible prophecy will clearly elucidate this role. I further believe that an enlightened understanding of Zechariah 12:10 is essential and throws clearer light on the subject.

RUACH HA KODESH

The Spirit referred to in Zechariah 12:10 is the *Ruach Ha Kodesh*— the Holy Spirit who is God. The prophet did not say, "I will pour out a spirit of grace...." He used the definite participle *the* Spirit (Ruach) of grace and supplications. There is a Trinitarian aspect to this Scripture in that one God is mentioned, but that mention is of three aspects of His being namely, God (Father), *Ruach Ha Kodesh* (Spirit), and Messiah. In the very simplest of examples, I Gerald Rowlands am a triune being yet one person—I am at the same time a son, husband, and father. Though I am actually only one person, I have three roles to fulfill. To my parents I remain their son. To my wife I am her husband, and to my children I am their father.

God predicts that He will pour upon the house of David and the inhabitants of Jerusalem His Holy Spirit who is wholly gracious, and who will elicit prayers and repentance from those on whom He is outpoured.

THE SPIRIT OF GRACE

Since the Holy Spirit is God, all the attributes and characteristics mentioned are valid expressions of His nature and character. Hence He may truly be called "The Spirit of grace." We may also understand that God's grace is always a prerequisite to salvation. Man cannot receive anything from God except by pure reason of His glorious grace. When the Spirit of grace is poured upon a person or people, all of God's abundance may be anticipated. Whenever God chooses to visit a people, that desire is always a product of His grace in which He makes Himself instantly and totally available to all who will turn to Him in faith and believe. When the Spirit of grace is therefore poured upon Israel as predicted, all of God's love, authority, and transforming power is made available to them.

Messiah also promises that when the Spirit comes, He will guide us into all truth (see John 8:32). I believe that modern Israel is in bondage to both pious religious tradition and modern human secularism. Centuries of suffering discrimination, persecution, and hardship have hardened their hearts rendering them brittle and vulnerable. It may be that many orthodox and religious Jews strive to fulfill every iota of the law sincerely believing that adherence to religious laws pleases God. How glorious it will be when the Holy Spirit of grace reveals that the just shall live by faith and the whole nation will be liberated from religious tradition into the true freedom of the children of God.

Israel has struggled alone throughout her long history when her people have been scattered worldwide. They have wandered pathways full of judgment, ostracism, and loneliness. But now the time of her resurrection is at hand. God is getting ready to glorify Himself in the eyes of all the nations through the mighty deliverance He will secure for Israel. When He has delivered them, He will cause a brand-new day to dawn for Israel. His glorious light will shine on her with such a powerful radiance that the whole world will clearly see the grace and glory of God upon His chosen people. He calls on Israel and Jerusalem to arise and shine with His glory.

AN IMMINENT FULFILLMENT?

The event shared in Zechariah 12:10 deserves a more thorough examination and investigation—its importance has long been greatly underestimated. I have never seen it expounded upon in this manner in any book on prophecy that I have read. Nor have I ever heard anyone teach about this most amazing prediction. Yet it is in the Bible and it would seem to be a possibility or even a probability to happen in the relatively near future. Certainly it may be the next major event on God's prophetic calendar.

I sincerely believe that the fulfillment of it will be an immensely important occasion, preceding the Rapture or the Second Coming and be equally as sensational. It is an event that involves a miraculous and astounding appearance of Christ to the nation of Israel and the outpouring of God's Spirit that will be even more amazing than on the Day of Pentecost. On that day, 120 men and women were baptized in the Holy Spirit and 3,000 people were converted. I believe that in a similar rapidly approaching event, an entire nation will be gloriously transformed.

Because the Church should be open to this possibility, I have searched Scripture and have provided the framework for you to consider, with an open heart and mind, whether it will happen or not. I urge you not to reject it out of hand or even neglect the need to urgently see if these things be so.

The first step is to better acquaint ourselves with the immense importance of Israel in God's end-time purposes and the fact that together with the Church, Israel has a truly amazing future. Those who believe that God has permanently finished with Israel need to think again and see that her role is intrinsic to the plan of redemption from Genesis to Revelation.

What if one of the most amazing predictions in the Bible is within range of imminent fulfillment and that its realization would completely transform Israel and ultimately the whole world scene? I have been considering that possibility prayerfully with great excitement, delving into the relevant Scriptures, searching for evidence that confirms or disproves this possibility.

I will pour out on the house of David and on the inhabitants of Jerusalem a spirit of grace and petition; and they shall look on Him whom they have thrust through, and they shall mourn for Him as one mourns for an only son, and they shall grieve over Him as one grieves over a first-born (Zechariah 12:10 NEB).

Another rendering of this in the Literal Translation Bible says, "and I will pour on the house of David and on those living in Jerusalem, the spirit of grace and prayer and they shall look on Me whom they have pierced and they shall mourn for Him as one mourns for an only son and they shall be bitter over Him like bitterness over a firstborn."

Questions this Scripture brings to mind include: Exactly what is this prophecy about? What will happen as a direct result of its fulfillment? When is it likely to happen?

Note that the preceding context of this chapter, Zechariah 12, predicts a war upon Israel and contains some very specific details of that war. Note also that immediately after and as a direct result of that war, God fulfills a sacred promise to Israel—the House of David. That promise is to pour out the *Ruach Ha Kodesh* (Holy Spirit) upon Israel and inhabitants of Jerusalem. This promise is reiterated in several places (see Isa. 44:3, 59:21; Ezek. 37:14, 39:29; Zech 12:10), but this particular portion mentions a number of specific results of the outpouring. This prophetic incident is preceded by an attack by all the immediate surrounding neighbors of Israel. It is no coincidence that all of these nations are now Muslim nations.

WHY ISRAEL AND JERUSALEM?

World attention is currently focused on the Middle East and particularly on Israel and Jerusalem. The United Nations, European Union, President Obama and his administration, together with the whole Muslim world seeks to force Israel into a peace process that I believe will lead to a massively destructive war. Israel is one of the smallest nations on earth, and Jerusalem is one of the smallest capital cities in the world. Why is the world uniting against tiny Israel, the only democracy in the Middle East? What is driving the frenzy of these nations as they strive to make Israel give room on her borders to a terrorist organization? To comply with the world's demands would be to commit national suicide and plunge the world into greater crises than ever. What is it about Israel and Jerusalem that attracts so much attention anger, bitterness, and strife? The following 10 answers to that question are for serious consideration:

1. Israel is the land of the Holy Bible where all the prophets lived and prophesied.
2. Israel is the place on earth that God has declared is uniquely "His."
3. Israel is the geographic center of the earth as far as the Bible is concerned.
4. Israel is the scene of Christ's birth, life, death, and resurrection.
5. Israel is the site of satan's defeat at the cross of Christ.
6. Israel is the birthplace of the Church in the city of Jerusalem.
7. Israel is the very place to which Christ will return to earth.
8. Jerusalem is the city in which the throne of Messiah will stand.
9. Israel will be the site from which Messiah will rule all nations.
10. Israel is the place where Zion is situated.

Over many centuries the meaning and application of the name *Zion* has often changed. It has frequently been applied to the city of Jerusalem, the people of Israel, and the land of Israel. However, it has never lost its original and main significance as the place where the throne of David was originally placed. Zion was recognized and renowned as the seat of government and justice. Since the throne of David did not only relate to David's reign but also to Messiah's reign, Zion has immensely important significance in God's prophetic plan.

Mount Zion was the precise spot where the throne of David was set, and it will be the very place from which Messiah will rule the nations. The Messiah comes from the ancestral line of David and will succeed to his throne.

DEFEATING THE ENEMIES OF ISRAEL

Many Christians cringe at the idea of God killing people, even the enemies of Israel; but the stark reality is that if these enemies are not killed, they will annihilate Israel. This is a matter of life, death, and national survival for Israel. They are under constant threat of annihilation and destruction. The annihilation of Israel and Jerusalem would completely destroy the integrity of God's Word. Jerusalem is absolutely integral to the return of Messiah and all the prophetic plans of God—this is precisely why extremist Islamic forces are determined to destroy the city.

> *In that day the LORD will defend the inhabitants of Jerusalem; the one who is feeble among them in that day shall be like David, and the house of David shall be like God, like the Angel of the LORD before them. It shall be in that day that I will seek to destroy all the nations that come against Jerusalem* (Zechariah 12:8-9 NKJV).

WHAT GOD IS SAYING

What God is saying in this verse is:

1. God will personally intervene to defend and rescue Israel and Jerusalem from her fanatical attackers.

2. The feeblest Jew, whether an infant or senior citizen, will be like King David, the warrior king of Israel.

3. The house of David will be like God Himself in strength, power, and authority.

4. The Angel of the Lord (Messiah) will personally lead Israel into battle.

5. God will destroy all the enemy armies that assault Jerusalem.

6. Jerusalem will remain fit for human habitation.

7. Messiah will reveal Himself and His true identity to Israel.

The prophet then proceeds to make the most thrilling declaration regarding His sovereign purpose for Israel—He predicts the new birth of Israel. Please notice that it is God Himself who is speaking and He says, "They shall look on *Me* whom they have pierced." The Jewish nation will have a direct revelation or view of their God. They will come face to face with Him. They will also see that He is the One who was pierced. They will finally recognize that the Man who was crucified outside Jerusalem, was actually the God of Israel in human form. They will also see that the One who has rescued them from total destruction and annihilation in the 21st century is actually the Jewish Messiah, in the palms of whose hands and side there are visible scars. They will also realize that the Messiah is God, the God of Israel. In fact, He is the Son of God and they will mourn over Him in a manner reserved for the death of one's only beloved son. *And they shall mourn for Him, as one mourns for his only son.*

What is God predicting in Zechariah 12:10? First of all He is saying that at the conclusion of the war that is waged upon Israel by her near neighbors, who are defeated because the Israel Defense Force is infused with the Spirit of God, the Lord of armies will win an amazing supernatural victory. A greater victory than they have won since the inception of the State of Israel. What is God declaring?

THE OUTPOURED SPIRIT (RUACH HA KODESH)

The outpoured Spirit consists of different and unique aspects. The following descriptions provide an understanding of each that I have discovered through research and personal revelation.

Spirit of Grace. Unmerited favor. Something that is not deserved but is a sovereign act of God's grace. I am not suggesting that somehow Israel is worthy of what God does for her. It is purely the grace of God and the timing of God and the purpose of God whereupon He will pour bounteously upon the nation His Holy Spirit of grace.

Spirit of Supplications. Prayers, pleading, and entreaty. This will not be a response to one prayer, but many prayers. Not prayers that are merely religious recitations, but desperate entreaties from deep within the soul of the nation.

Spirit of Revelation. Jesus said, "Holy Spirit will show you all things" (John 14:26). This glorious outpouring of the Holy Spirit will bring to Israel a new revelation of the person of Messiah.

Spirit of Mourning and Regret for the Messiah's death. The whole nation of Israel will suddenly understand that when Christ died on the cross it was the death of God's son. The nation will mourn with greater mourning and regret than has ever been manifest.

Spirit of Repentance (sadness, remorse and change of heart and belief). Their repentance will be sadness and deep regret, but also a change of heart and belief. This spirit of repentance will be manifest throughout the whole State of Israel.

Spirit of Private and Personal Concern. Families apart. The Scripture says that families will grieve apart from one another. Husbands and wives will grieve apart from each other. (See Zechariah 12:11.)

Spirit of National Mourning and sadness that's comes upon the entire nation.

Spirit of Forgiveness and Cleansing. "In that day a fountain shall be opened for the house of David and for the inhabitants of Jerusalem, for sin and for uncleanness" (Zech. 13:1 NKJV). This type of mourning is reserved for royalty. Like the death of King Josiah at Hadad Rimmon after 30 years of peace, prosperity, and major beneficial reform, who was buried in Jerusalem amid great mourning and sadness throughout all Israel and Jerusalem. Josiah was one of Judah's greatest kings. In many ways he was a type of the Messiah.

An Amazing Prediction

*And I will pour on the house of David, **and on the inhabitants** [people] of Jerusalem, the spirit of grace and of prayers* (Zechariah 12:10 NKJV).

The prophet Zechariah does not say "on the House of David **even the people** (inhabitants) of Jerusalem" but specifically **"*and on* the inhabitants of Jerusalem."** This intimates two separate groups of people. Today's inhabitants of Jerusalem are not only Jews, there are also Christians and Muslims residing there. Is God declaring that He will also pour out the Holy Spirit in grace, supplications, and revelation to Jews, Christians, and Muslims in Jerusalem? I believe this may well be so, and that it will constitute a new era and fresh outpouring as predicted by the prophet Joel that will encompass these three people groups who are all seed of Abraham. In a world in which the greatest problem is the animosity between Muslim and non-Muslim nations, how brilliant is a strategy through which God will produce a unity in Jerusalem that may quickly spread throughout the whole earth?

The living God, who powerfully delivered Israel from Egypt and led them miraculously through the wilderness and into the Promised Land, withdrew His living presence from Israel. He returned to His place until they would acknowledge their offence and diligently seek His face. He predicted that in their affliction they would earnestly seek Him (see Hosea 5:15, 6:1-3). That day is about to dawn for Israel and with it a glorious era of peace and prosperity that will make her the envy of all nations.

The Redeemer From Zion

"The Redeemer will come to Zion, and to those who turn from transgression in Jacob," says the LORD (Isaiah 59:20 NKJV).

The Redeemer will come first to Zion and those of Jacob who turn from their transgressions. Then He will turn to the nations with salvation. (See Isaiah 45:22-25.)

IMPORTANT STATEMENT OF JESUS

O Jerusalem, Jerusalem, the city that kills the prophets and stones God's messengers! How often I have wanted to gather your children together as a hen protects her chicks beneath her wings, but you wouldn't let Me. And now look, your house is left to you, empty and desolate. For I tell you this, you will never see Me again until you say, "Blessings on the One who comes in the name of the Lord!"(Matthew 23:37-39).

Please notice in these truths:

1. Jesus spoke directly to the rulers of Jerusalem.
2. He spoke of His great yearning to protect them.
3. Their house (rule) would be left desolate for a season.
4. Verse 39 did *not* say Israel would never see Him again.
5. It is predicted that they would see Him again.
6. Verse 39 could be translated, "You *will* see Me again when you say Blessed is He who comes in the name of the Lord."
7. They would see Him in Jerusalem.

A great outpouring of the Holy Spirit and spiritual harvest will take place following Messiah's appearance to Israel. It will come first upon Israel and then all the nations on earth (see Joel 2:28-32).

What these prophetic statements declare is truly exciting but even more challenging is the fact that the war that precedes this amazing event is already engaged in its earliest stages. The sworn enemies of Israel residing in all her neighboring nations are preparing for the next stage of the assault. This local war which was recently fought in Gaza in 2008-2009, will become a full blown war; and despite all the diplomatic talks, it will finally manifest itself as an extremely powerful attack apparently capable of annihilating Israel. This will be the signal for Messiah's direct intervention. I believe that this war will immediately precede the revelation of the Messiah to the Jewish people.

This is an extremely critical time in world history. It is a time for every Bible believer to enter the fray through serious and intentional intercession and prayers on behalf of Israel. Not only is Israel's reputation and security at stake, the reputation of the One who calls Himself the "Holy One of Israel" is also at stake.

God's grace, mercy, and loving-kindness toward Israel has never been withdrawn. There have been many times when Israel has been unable to recognize or discern His presence, but He has been there nevertheless. In the last days of this era, God's grace will triumph on the behalf of Israel—He will display His loyalty before the whole world. Every nation on earth will recognize and acknowledge that the Jews of Israel are the chosen people of God.

Chapter Three

"...FOR THE JEW FIRST..."

Several important themes run through the Bible. One of these subjects is called the "Jew First Principle." Paul mentions this briefly in Romans 1,

> *For I am not ashamed of the gospel of Christ, for it is the power of God to salvation for everyone who believes, **for the Jew first** and also for the Greek* [Gentile]. *For in it the righteousness of God is revealed from faith to faith; as it is written, "The just shall live by faith"* (Romans 1:16-17 NKJV).

The biblical principle by which Paul states "to the Jew first" does not only apply to the preaching of the gospel as per the situation in Romans 1:16, it is also a principle traceable throughout the Bible from Genesis to Revelation. In the great plan of redemption, Israel is seen as the "Elder Brother" of the redeemed community. In the structure of a properly functioning family, the eldest brother has certain privileges, particularly with regard to his inheritance. However, it is also true that he has added responsibilities to his father and his family.

THE JEW FIRST PRINCIPLE

Throughout the Bible there are consistent instances when God visited the children of Israel first before any other nation. Examples include:

- In Egypt when He delivered them from Pharaoh. (See Exodus 13.)

- At Mount Sinai when He gave the commandments to humankind. (See Exodus 20.)

- With the prophets to whom He delivered His Word— Zechariah, Joel, Isaiah, etc.

- Jews were first ordained as Levitical priests to serve God. (See Exodus 19:22; 28:1,4,41; 29:1,9,44; 30:30, etc.)

- At Pentecost when Joel's prophecy began to be fulfilled. (See Acts 2 and Joel 2.)

- At the fulfillment of Zechariah 12:10 and the Joel 2 outpouring.

- In Revelation 7:4-8 where God sealed the twelve tribes of Israel. This fact is mentioned prior to the innumerable company.

Since God has always followed the Jew First Principle, is it not feasible and probable that He will continue it forever?

The fact of being "God's chosen people" has been seen by some Jews as an onerous burden rather than a desirable privilege. Throughout history some Jews, just like Tevye in *Fiddler on the Roof*, have wished that God had chosen another people and nation to be His special people. For God has not only promised blessings first to obedient Israel, He has also threatened judgments first for disobedience—this has often been the lot of Israel. Paul refers to this, citing tribulation, anguish, indignation, and wrath as the alternative to glory, honor, and immortality.

First in Judgment and Blessing

God promised blessings for obedience, but He also predicted judgment for disobedience. Israel has frequently been the object of divine punishment because of her disobedience. God made the threat and has fulfilled it throughout history. He is faithful to His Word as well as His promises of great blessings in the time when the nation of Israel will unanimously repent and be converted.

Eternal life to those who by patient continuance in doing good seek for glory, honor, and immortality; but to those who are self-seeking

*and do not obey the truth, but obey unrighteousness—indigna-
tion and wrath, tribulation and anguish, on every soul of man
who does evil, of the Jew first and also of the Greek; but glory,
honor, and peace to everyone who works what is good, **to the Jew
first** and also to the Greek. For there is no partiality with God*
(Romans 2:7-11 NKJV).

For many centuries the scattered Jewish people have painfully
experienced such tribulation but this will soon end, and God will
bestow glory, honor, and immortality upon them. To the degree that
they have suffered in the past, they will be honored with a double
portion of blessing. For whatever humiliation they have suffered,
God will give them double that in honor. I believe this is what God
refers to in Isaiah 40:

*Speak comfort to Jerusalem, and cry out to her, that her warfare
is ended, that her iniquity is pardoned; for she has received from
the LORD's hand double for all her sins* (Isaiah 40:2 NKJV).

PRIORITY FOR THE JEWS

In what ways do the Jews have priority? Paul poses this intriguing question in Romans 3 and answers his own question.

*What advantage then has the Jew, or what is the profit of cir-
cumcision? Much in every way!* (Romans 3:1-2 NKJV)

In the Middle Eastern culture of the Bible, the first, and therefore eldest, son occupied a very special place in the family structure. A particularly special position of respect was attributed to
him. No matter how many siblings he eventually had, the firstborn maintained a unique and privileged place in his father's eyes.
Therefore, the special and unique relationship that God has with
Israel is underlined and emphasized in that God calls that nation
"My firstborn son" (Exod. 4:22). This honor and respect is continued, even throughout the centuries in which Israel is placed to
one side in order to grant the Gentiles access to God's family. God
has never deserted or disowned Israel. He has never withdrawn
from them their special status before Him. His love for them has
never wavered or diminished. I believe that His intent has always

been to regather them, restore them, and renew Israel's place of honor among the nations.

Israel Is God's Firstborn Son

God commanded Moses to tell Pharaoh that Israel is His first-born son,

> *Then you shall say to Pharaoh, "Thus says the LORD: 'Israel is My son, My firstborn'"* (Exodus 4:22).

The Law of the Firstborn Son

The Greek word for *first* is "proton."[1]

Proton can specify time, meaning "first in time, earliest" in a sequence of events. It also intimates first in time, place, order, and importance. Proton can also mean rank or degree, "first, foremost, most important, most prominent" or "in the first place, above all, especially." This can imply a priority of position, or being first in an order of priorities. As Christian believers, Israel is our Elder Brother who comes first.

In ancient Israel, the property of a deceased person was usually distributed according to law or tribal custom. Written wills were rarely used. The real and personal property of a father was normally divided among his sons. A larger amount, usually a double portion, went to the eldest son, who assumed the care of his mother and unmarried sisters (see Deut. 21:15-17; 1 Chronicles 5:1).

Moses spoke of a situation in which a man had two wives and the second wife was for various reasons the favorite wife, probably being younger and more comely (see Deut. 21:15).

The case of Jacob and his two wives, Leah and Rachel, illustrates this situation. Although Rachel was Jacob's favorite wife, the line of David and ultimately the Messiah, passed through Leah and her son Judah, not Rachel. Leah was the less-favored of the two wives of Jacob, and she must have been painfully conscious of this during the years of her marriage. But it was Leah rather than Rachel who gave birth to Judah, through whose line Jesus the Messiah was eventually born (see Matt. 1:2).

Many churchmen throughout the centuries, through the introduction of human and often pagan religious traditions, have successfully separated the Church from its original Hebraic roots. However, God has determined to rectify this error by re-grafting Israel's branches onto their own tree (see Rom. 11:23) Christians should remember that from Israel has come every blessing and privilege that we enjoy (see Rom. 9:4-5).

In Exodus 4:22, the LORD calls Israel His firstborn son. This statement in a nutshell reveals the place of Israel in God's grand design for humanity. In Old Testament society, the firstborn son received the birthright. He had priority and authority over all his brothers. He received the greatest share of his father's wealth. Spiritually, Israel was God's firstborn son. They were to be foremost among the nations. From Israel was to spring the Messiah, the King of Israel first, and then of all nations. The Twelve Tribes of Israel are once again mentioned first and given due prominence in chapter 7:5-8 in the Book of Revelation. Is God planning to restore them to their position of spiritual priority?

To the Hebrew mind, the term *inheritance* had strong spiritual and national connotations extending far beyond the family estate. The land of Canaan was regarded as an inheritance from the Lord because God had promised the land to Abraham and his descendants (see Num. 33:53). Both Moses and Joshua were told by the Lord to divide the land of Canaan among the tribes "as an inheritance" (Num. 26:52-53; Josh. 13:6). God directed that the land be distributed to each tribe by lot according to its population. Proton does not necessarily suggest better or superior, but rather first in line to one's inheritance.

ISRAEL—THE FIRST COVENANT PEOPLE

I have also established My covenant with them, to give them the land of Canaan, the land of their pilgrimage, in which they were strangers. And I have also heard the groaning of the children of Israel whom the Egyptians keep in bondage, and I have remembered My covenant (Exodus 6:4-5 NKJV).

ISRAEL—THE ORIGINAL CHOSEN PEOPLE OF GOD

For you are a holy people to the LORD your God, and the LORD has chosen you to be a people for Himself, a special treasure above all the peoples who are on the face of the earth (Deuteronomy 14:2 NKJV).

CHOSEN BECAUSE OF HIS LOVE

God's sovereign love, His freedom to choose whom He would love, is the reason He chose Israel above all other nations. Who can understand or explain the choice of a lover? (See Deuteronomy 7:6-8.)

GOD'S LITMUS TEST

A litmus test is a simple procedure to test the chemical constituency of a particular liquid substance to determine whether it is acidic or alkaline. It is a test for chemical acidity using a special paper—litmus paper. When litmus paper is dipped into a liquid chemical substance, it will turn either blue or red depending on the chemical composition of the liquid.

This phrase may also refer to something regarded as a simple and accurate test of a particular thing, such as a person's attitude to a specific issue. I personally believe that part of God's purpose in choosing the Jews to be His special people on earth was to use them as a litmus test for humanity. Jews today are very much what the nations have made them over many centuries by their various attitudes toward them. Like all people, Jews can be good or bad, nice or nasty depending to some extent on their circumstances and how they are either received or rejected. Reaction to Jews, whether positive or negative, will one day determine whether a particular people are regarded as sheep or goats. (See Matthew 25:32-33.)

THE PRICE OF ELECTION

Israel's election was for the sake of the nations, to be "a light to the nations" (Isa. 42:6, 49:6, 51:4, 60:1-3; Acts 13:47). She was the vehicle by which God would bring the Scriptures and the Savior to the world. The people of Israel—the Jewish people—have suffered greatly because of this election. It is from the bloody womb of Israel that the Church was born. Paul reveals his primary and enduring love and concern for his Jewish brethren. Like his ancestor Moses, he himself would rather be blotted out from God's book than see his fellow countrymen erased from it (see Rom. 9:3-5).

MESSIAH'S ORIGINAL COMMISSION

*And now the LORD speaks—He who formed me in my mother's womb to be His servant , **who commissioned me to bring His people of Israel back to Him**. The LORD has honored me, and my God has given me strength. **He says, "You will do more than restore the people of Israel to Me. I will make you a light to the Gentiles, and you will bring My salvation to the ends of the earth"*** (Isaiah 49:5-6).

THE COMMISSION OF THE MESSIAH

The Commission of the Messiah was to first "bring His people of Israel back to Him." Then second, to be a "light to the Gentiles" and take His "salvation to the ends of the earth" (Isa. 49:5-6).

Throughout the years, many Christians have conveniently overlooked the fact that in the original commissioning that Jehovah gave to the Messiah, His primary task was to bring the people of Israel back to Him. Since the 3rd century, in Constantine's day, the church has sadly and badly neglected this sacred entrusted task. Messiah also commissioned His disciples to do the same thing.

THROUGH DIVINE REVELATION

Then He [Jesus] *asked them, "Who do you say I am?" Simon Peter answered, "**You are the Messiah**, the Son of the living God"* (Matthew 16:15-16).

The recognition of who Jesus truly was came to Peter purely through divine revelation, not through any human reasoning. He did not simply deduce by logic that Jesus was the promised Messiah. The revelation came directly from the Father in Heaven. The English rendering of this verse in many Bible versions, "You are the Christ!" diminishes the implications of the statement. The revelation that Peter received concerning the Messiah validated all the Jewish prophetic predictions regarding the One who was to come, the long promised Messiah of Israel. The revelation confirmed and authenticated the Messiah's Jewish hereditary connection. It is precisely because of this connection to historic Israel that we recipients of Jesus have also inherited Jewish citizenship (see Eph. 2:18-19).

THE ANTICIPATED KINGDOM

The Jewish people were longing for deliverance from Roman oppression. They were looking for the promised redeemer who they believed would liberate the nation. Sadly they failed to recognize that Zechariah's prophecy would be fulfilled in two phases.

> *Rejoice greatly, O daughter of Zion! Shout, O daughter of Jerusalem! Behold, your King is coming to you; He is just and having salvation, lowly and riding on a donkey, a colt, the foal of a donkey. I will cut off the chariot from Ephraim and the horse from Jerusalem; the battle bow shall be cut off. He shall speak peace to the nations; His dominion shall be "from sea to sea, and from the River to the ends of the earth"* (Zechariah 9:9-10 NKJV).

In the amazing vision that John was given of future events, including the ingathering of a vast company into the Kingdom of God, the first sight he saw was of a large group of 144,000 Jews whom God had divinely sealed. I do not think that 144,000 is meant to be a mathematically precise number. I believe it is a symbolic number. It first represents all the twelve tribes of Israel and second, twelve is the number of divine government.

SEALING THE 144,000 JEWS

> *And I heard the number of those who were sealed. One hundred and forty-four thousand of all the tribes of the children of Israel were sealed* (Revelation 7:4 NKJV).

When John turned his gaze from the 144,000 Jews, he immediately saw in the same context another company, this time a vast innumerable multitude of Gentile believers. The phrase "which no man could number" intimates a crowd so large that its accurate number could not be visually estimated.

> *After these things I looked, and behold, a great multitude which no one could number, of all nations, tribes, peoples, and tongues, standing before the throne and before the Lamb, clothed with white robes, with palm branches in their hands, and crying out with a loud voice, saying, "Salvation belongs to our God who sits on the throne, and to the Lamb!" All the angels stood around the throne and the elders and the four living creatures, and fell on their faces before the throne and worshiped God, saying: "Amen! Blessing and glory and wisdom, Thanksgiving and honor and power and might, be to our God forever and ever. Amen"* (Revelation 7:9-12 NKJV).

THE ETERNAL KINGDOM OF DAVID

> *Now it shall come to pass in the latter days that the mountain of the LORD's house shall be established on the top of the mountains, and shall be exalted above the hills; and all nations shall flow to it. Many people shall come and say, "Come, and let us go up to the mountain of the LORD, to the house of the God of Jacob; He will teach us His ways, and we shall walk in His paths." For out of Zion shall go forth the law, and the word of the LORD from Jerusalem* (Isaiah 2:2-3 NKJV).

The Kingdom of God is not a vague, abstract, or ethereal myth like Camelot. It is real. Its capital and throne will be in Jerusalem—in a tangible, physical city of Jerusalem.

ENDNOTE

1. Strong's Concordance.

Chapter Four

CLEAR AND PRESENT DANGER

The pages of human history are stained with the blood of a multitude of wars, every one of which has left a legacy of bereavement and loss. The sad consequences of some of these wars have lingered for centuries, negatively influencing the lives of millions of people and causing devastating effects that have blighted entire nations. How tragic that unregenerate man does not learn the painful lessons of history. It should be very clear by now that another world-shattering battle will soon take place that will change the international landscape forever. Rogue nations are determined to obtain highly destructive weapons. Huge amounts of money and resources that could be used to feed the poor and starving are being used instead to produce and stockpile nuclear weapons.

The Church of Jesus Christ constitutes the particular body of humanity that should be most conscious of this soon-coming event because it is clearly foretold and predicted in the Bible. Christians should be a people that not only recognize the inevitability of this war but they should also be the advance guard of those who prepare themselves to take positive action to take full advantage of the universal debacle that will flow in the wake of this war. The greatest spiritual harvest in human history will take place following this earth-shattering event.

STRONG INDICATORS

Several indications give strong evidence for those whose minds are not closed to reality of the inevitability and near proximity of this war.

Bible Prophecies

Numerous prophetic scenarios in the Bible predict the expected war launched by the close neighbours of Israel in the "Last Day." Such a war is distinctly different to predictions in both Ezekiel 38 and 39, or that of Armageddon. The alliance of nations described is quite different. The unfolding result and time frame is also distinctly different. Relatively few Bible commentators have identified this war, and thus the Church and the world is largely ignorant concerning this war and its shocking impending effects. In several parts of prophetic Scripture, forecasts are made of a war upon Israel in the last days. This war is described in considerable detail and the devastating results are very clear. (See Psalm 83, Joel 3, Zechariah 12.)

Numerous Bible commentators would have us believe that these prophecies were fulfilled in the historic past, but the fact that in many instances total destruction is described proves they have not yet been fulfilled. It is amazing to see how accurate these descriptions are, though mostly delivered around 2,500 years ago. We will look at a number of these predictions later. The predictions are an indication of the intense anger of God particularly toward nations that have set themselves toward destroying the Jewish people and their nation. The biblical prophecies regarding the destruction of Damascus, Tyre, and Sidon, Gaza, and others cannot possibly have been historically fulfilled because those cities and places are still in existence.

Islamic Determination

The resolve and determination of militant Islamic factions is vicious, unrelenting, and growing continually. I believe that this resolve and determination is grossly underestimated throughout the non-Muslim world. Evidence is found all over Europe where a quiet invasion of Muslims through immigration has been going on for years.[1] The demographic map of Europe is being slowly but relentlessly changed as Muslim populations expand. This transformation is not by chance. It is a well-planned, expensively organized stealth strategy. Many nations in Europe now have an Islamic "fifth column" firmly established in their midst capable of asserting religious control in the relatively near future. In addition to the quiet invasion by immigration, thousands of fanatical extremists are dedicated to raining death and destruction on all "infidels" (non-Muslims). They have committed their lives to suicide attacks on civilians and military alike. A tragic example of this is the devout Muslim U.S. Army colonel who opened fire at Fort Hood, Texas, killing 13 and wounding 30 others at the military base.[2]

ISLAMIC PROPHECY

Islamic prophecies concerning the Last Days predict a monumental battle between the forces of Islam and those of Israel and the rest of the world. Predictions from the Hadith[3] declare that all Muslims will launch a great war against the Jews and thoroughly defeat them. The prophecy says that the Last Day will not dawn until the Muslims fight the Jews and wrest from them the Holy Land. The Muslims will be granted decisive victory over the Jews. The prophecy details that the rocks and trees will say, "Oh Muslim. Oh Servant of Allah, there are Jews behind me, come and kill them!" During this massive battle, Jerusalem is said to be destroyed.

Such predictions are thoroughly disputed in Bible prophecies in which Israel is granted overwhelming victory over her Muslim assailants, and Jerusalem is protected and delivered from their violent attack. Not only will Jerusalem remain inhabitable, it will also be glorified by the presence of God and will experience a period of peace, prosperity, and enviable development. Jerusalem will be an international center of world attention and admiration.

ISRAEL IS PREPARING: IS THE CHURCH?

Israel is already taking various practical, precautionary measures to deal with the threat of imminent war, but there are few signs that the Church is preparing for the reality and aftermath of this soon-to-come war. If we imagine for one moment that the threat is Israel's problem alone, we are making a massive error of judgment. Although the threat is initially toward Israel, it will subsequently become an issue affecting the whole world.

The Church worldwide will be soon faced with a tremendous challenge when Zechariah 12:10 is fulfilled. The challenges and opportunities that will fall to the Church will require an entirely new perception and strategy. The traditional Church and particularly its Western-influenced traditions will not suffice to meet the challenge that it will face. It will particularly need to change its attitude toward Israel as God brings Jew and Gentile together in the One New Man that Paul predicted. There will be a phenomenal harvest to reap from all the nations on earth that will be impossible to achieve unless the Church as well as Israel is totally transformed.

Christians who hold a traditional view of End Times, the Rapture, the Great Tribulation, and the Second Coming will doubtless wonder how and where these suggested events fit into the timeline.

I believe that the revelation of Messiah's identity to His original chosen people will initiate the period of relative peace that Israel is said to experience in Ezekiel 38. It will be the commencement of the period introduced in Isaiah 60 when the glory of the Lord will arise upon Israel and all the nations, including several Muslim nations, will acknowledge that Yaweh the supreme God, is with His people Israel.

Arise, Jerusalem, and shine like the sun; the glory of the LORD is shining on you! Other nations will be covered by darkness, but on you the light of the LORD will shine; the brightness of His presence will be with you. Nations will be drawn to your light, and kings to the dawning of your day (Isaiah 60:1-3 GNT).

At the conclusion of this peaceful period, the war of Ezekiel 38 and 39 will take place when once again God will win a devastating victory. I believe that this will lead into the Great Tribulation during which time a great multitude of Jews and Gentiles will enter the fold and Kingdom of God, the Great Shepherd. Finally at the close of the Tribulation, Armageddon will take place after which the nations will enter the Millennium.

I humbly challenge any Bible student, when studying Zechariah 12:10 in conjunction with its full immediate context, to place any alternative interpretation on this Scripture than the one I am suggesting. The entire context of the chapter is obviously and indisputably an end-time scenario. The Holy Spirit is poured out upon the nation of Israel eliciting petitions and prayers of repentance and sorrow toward the One on whom their gaze is fixed. This person is the Messiah Himself, and the nation is transformed by the divinely arranged interaction between them and their Messiah.

I believe that the age in which we now live will come to a conclusion with the Psalm 83 war. Everything will then change for the church and the world. This dramatic change will eventuate because God will exalt Israel to a place of international pre-eminence. I believe that Israel will then begin a period of peace and remarkable prosperity and will also become a Messianic nation.

This peaceful era may last for some years, but eventually Gog and Magog will bring it to another climax by launching another attack upon Israel (see Ezek. 38 and 39). Once again God will triumph over the enemies of Israel, but following this war the world will experience the Great Tribulation which will last for seven years until the battle of Armageddon.

Jehovah indicates the strategy His people should adopt in case of enemy attacks.

> *When you go out to battle against your enemies, and see horses and chariots and people more numerous than you, do not be afraid of them; for the LORD your God is with you, who brought you up from the land of Egypt. So it shall be, when you are on the verge of battle, that the priest shall approach and speak to the people. And he shall say to them, "Hear, O Israel: Today you are on the verge of battle with your enemies. Do not let your heart faint, do not be afraid, and do not tremble or be terrified because of them; for the LORD your God is He who goes with you, to fight for you against your enemies, to save you"* (Deuteronomy 20:1-4 NKJV).

His strategy includes:

1. When confronted by enemy armies larger than Israel's army and much better equipped, Israel is not to retreat

but to advance. "Go out to battle against them" is God's explicit instruction.

2. Do not be afraid of them, for Jehovah, the very same God who delivered you from an impossible situation in Egypt, is with you with the same authority and power as He exercised then.

3. On the verge of the battle, the priests (spiritual leaders) are to speak to the people. Their exhortation should be "don't be afraid, tremble, or be terrified, for Jehovah your God goes with you to fight against your enemies."

4. The sole intention of Jehovah is to give victory and to save them from their enemies. If Israel obeys God's exhortations, He guarantees them victory!

THE KINGDOM BEGINS TO EMERGE

When Jesus commenced His ministry, He began by proclaiming the proximity of the Kingdom (see Mark 1:14). Peter was also given the "keys of the Kingdom" (Matt. 16:19) and used those keys on the Day of Pentecost. Now by the grace of God we have been translated into the Kingdom if we live under the rule of the King. However, the Kingdom has not yet appeared in its fullest sense.

Jesus spoke about the Kingdom of God many times. It was, perhaps, His favorite topic. At times, He said, "The Kingdom is here," while at other times, He proclaimed, "The Kingdom is coming." So, which is it? Theologians call this conundrum the "now and not yet" Kingdom; in other words, it's a paradox. It's both. The Kingdom has come with the emergence of the Church; but at the same time, Jesus is returning to reign supremely as King and to establish His Kingdom on earth from His throne in Jerusalem.

Following the predicted destruction of Israel's enemies in the "Last Day" battle for Jerusalem, the authority of the Kingdom of God will be manifested in a more dramatic and powerful manner than ever before. This manifestation will begin when the Messiah reveals His true identity to the house of David. Jewish prayers for Messiah's appearance will finally be answered. The Angel of the

Lord, the Messiah, will personally lead the Israelis into battle and win for them an amazing supernatural victory (see Zech. 12:8-10). Israel and all the nations of the world will stand in awe of the triumphant Messiah. Israel's spiritual blindness will be healed in a moment and from that nation will emerge thousands of Messianic believers who will combine together with Gentile believers in reaping the greatest harvest ever. This company will be augmented by large groups of former Muslims whose allegiance will be transferred to Jehovah and His Messiah.

All of Israel's Muslim neighbors consistently threaten Israel with total destruction. It is obvious that such a war will impact dramatically upon the world. The power behind the present threat is Iran. Iran is also the prime motivator and strategist of the upheaval in the Palestinian ranks.

What these forces of evil do not realize as they encourage themselves with sweet thoughts of victory is that they are not only challenging the military might of Israel. They are also pitting their strength against the God of the Bible. His response will be of apocalyptic proportion as He fulfills His promise to protect and defend His chosen people in the land that He has vouchsafed to them so frequently and consistently throughout the Bible.

I believe the next major event to befall our world will be initiated by the fierce attack launched upon Israel by her surrounding Arab neighbors. This will be a war with several amazing results including the annexing by Israel of large pieces of territory that are presently under Arab control:

> *This is what the LORD says: "You will rule the Egyptians, the Ethiopians, and the Sabeans. They will come to you with all their merchandise and it will all be yours. They will follow you as prisoners in chains. They will fall to their knees in front of you and say, 'God is with you, and He is the only God. There is no other'"* (Isaiah 45:14).

However, another result will be the drastic destabilization of the world as a direct consequence of the war. The Western world will be paralyzed by a severe lack of oil and financial income. It is my opinion that as a possible consequence of the Arab defeat, the world's economy will completely collapse and the cost of goods and services will rise dramatically.

For the universal Church of Jesus Christ and all the nations on earth, it is time to realize that we are living on the very edge of predicted apocalyptic events. The threats of Islam are an irresistible unrelenting force, and the promises of God constitute a seemingly immovable object. The obvious determination and strategy of Israel's enemies is such that there may be no military defense system that can adequately cope with their attack. It will require a supernatural, divine intervention to prevent annihilation and devastating desolation. This will be a clash of unimaginable proportions. If God does not defend and deliver Israel from her sworn enemies, His self-acclaimed title of The Holy One of Israel and the Lord of Heaven's armies, will be meaningless. The many assurances that God has given concerning the protection of Israel, if not fulfilled, will render His promises unreliable and His character seriously flawed. Thank God His promises will never fail. He will come to the aid and defense of Israel according to His Word. (See Isaiah 44:21-23 and Jeremiah 10:6-7.)

Sounding the Trumpet

I want to blow the loudest trumpet call possible to awaken a Church that is, for the most part, in a deep sleep, oblivious to the significance of events that are presently happening around the world and particularly in the Middle East. I earnestly pray to grab the attention of all Christians and shout into their ears the warning of a huge impending event. Even though many prophetic signs concerning the future are now being fulfilled, many preachers and churches remain silent about anything remotely connected to the End Times and the Second Coming of Jesus.

With regard to Bible prophecy, the majority of church leaders are like ostriches with their heads in the sand while their congregations remain in a state of woeful ignorance of End Times. However, this state of affairs will soon come to an end when an imminent war in the Middle East breaks out and shatters our ear drums. The whole world will then change dramatically never to be the same again as it rushes headlong into a confrontation with Almighty God. So-called "peace treaties" and "roadmaps to peace" are worthless. It is futile to appeal to the good will of Israel's enemies. They have no moral ethics when it comes to dialogues, diplomacy, and conferences. They consider that participation in such efforts is a sign of weakness and vulnerability.

It is tragic and ironic to see that for the most part only the religious groups that are seen by many to be false cults are blowing a prophetic trumpet of warning concerning the End Times and impending judgment. Most Evangelical, Charismatic, and Pentecostal churches appear to be totally absorbed in self-serving teachings that tickle the ears of carnal men.

WE ARE CHILDREN OF THE LIGHT— WALK IN IT

Paul sends a clear message to the church in Thessalonica that is important for us to remember today:

> *But you, brethren, are not in darkness, so that this Day should overtake you as a thief. You are all sons of light and sons of the day. We are not of the night nor of darkness. Therefore let us not sleep, as others do, but let us watch and be sober. For those who sleep, sleep at night, and those who get drunk are drunk at night. But let us who are of the day be sober, putting on the breastplate of faith and love, and as a helmet the hope of salvation. For God did not appoint us to wrath, but to obtain salvation through our Lord Jesus Christ, who died for us, that whether we wake or sleep, we should live together with Him. Therefore comfort each other and edify one another, just as you also are doing* (1 Thessalonians 5:4-11 NKJV).

Paul further exhorts in Second Timothy:

> *But know this, that in the last days perilous times will come: For men will be lovers of themselves, lovers of money, boasters, proud, blasphemers, disobedient to parents, unthankful, unholy, unloving, unforgiving, slanderers, without self-control, brutal, despisers of good, traitors, headstrong, haughty, lovers*

of pleasure rather than lovers of God, having a form of godliness but denying its power. And from such people turn away! (2 Timothy 3:1-5 NKJV)

Second Timothy 3:2-4 describe the signs and symptoms of humanism in contrast to true Christian ethics. It appears that much of the Church in the Last Days will be humanistic with an outer layer (form) of godliness. Paul warns that the spirit of the age will invade churches and even many Christians will become:

1. Lovers of self. Teaching doctrines that benefit selfish desires.
2. Lovers of money. Emphasizing a message of material prosperity.
3. Proud boasters. Self-sufficient.
4. Unthankful. Lacking gratitude.
5. Unholy. Manifesting the sins of the flesh, rather than the fruit of the Spirit.
6. Unloving. Lacking true compassion for others.
7. Lovers of pleasure more than lovers of God.
8. Having a form (outward appearance) of godliness but not the power thereof.

ARE WE READY?

We need to be awake to the words of Jesus in Matthew 24:44 (NKJV), "Therefore you also be ready, for the Son of Man is coming at an hour you do not expect."

It seems obvious to me that very few churches today really expect the return of Christ to happen in the imminent future. Ironically, this is the very time that He will do so. The Bible says, "At such an hour that you do not expect Him, He will appear!" Our minds need to be focused on the Word of God and the many signs taking place around us that Jesus said would indicate that His return is close at hand.

One of the major signs is the re-birth of Israel in the Promised Land. In association with that, numerous other signs will also be in evidence, one of which may well be the scenario predicted in Psalm 83.

Most Bible commentators and students of eschatology have presumed that there are only two major End Times wars predicted in the Bible. They see a war as described in Ezekiel 38 and 39 taking place first, preceding the Tribulation; and then the Battle of Armageddon taking place at the close of the Great Tribulation.

Could it be that the Bible predicts another war that will take place before Ezekiel 38? Is this the war spoken of in Psalm 83 and other parts of Scripture? There are many prophetic passages, particularly concerning Israel's near neighbors, which obviously do not fit into the Ezekiel pattern. I must admit that the prophetic perspective of Psalm 83 fits with my spirit. It offers more than a single ray of hope for Israel's immediate future that causes my heart to rejoice. It suggests a reprieve for Israel followed by a most remarkable and thrilling period when Messianic messengers will come forth from Israel in astonishing numbers.

> *In that day Jerusalem will be known as The Throne of the LORD. All nations will come there to honor the LORD. They will no longer stubbornly follow their own evil desires. In those days the people of Judah and Israel will return together from exile in the north. They will return to the land I gave their ancestors as an inheritance forever* (Jeremiah 3:17-18).

The phrase "in that day" refers to the time frame that occurs at the end time of this present age and not specifically to a millennial age. Jeremiah 3:17-18 says that Jerusalem will be known as the throne of God in those days when the people of Judah and Israel return to the land that God gave to their ancestors as an eternal inheritance. See also Jeremiah 17:12-13 and Jeremiah 31:16-17.

MILLENNIAL MINDSET

In many of the numerous prophecies of redemption for Israel, there is no specific reference that would link their fulfillment to a millennial period. Nevertheless, most Christian commentators have assumed that all such promises will be fulfilled in the Millennium when the Messiah will assume His role as the King of kings and

Lord of lords. He will then rule over Israel and the nations of the world (see Isaiah 44:6; 47:4).

Many Bible scholars disagree as to which nations will align themselves against Israel in Ezekiel 38, there is much disagreement as to who Gog and Magog are. In Ezekiel 38:3 we are told that Gog is the prince of Rosh. This may refer to the ruling power of Russia, which is still a communist-thinking country although it made a painful switch from a communist to a free market economy in the 1990s. However, it is also becoming very apparent that Islam will soon constitute a major force in greater Russia and the nations to the south who are former members of the U.S.S.R. This future alliance of nations will very probably include Turkey.

God threatens to bring all these powers to judgment. Hooks are only placed into the jaws of animals that are being brought to the slaughter house. God describes Russia and her immediate allies, Meshech and Tubal, representing the communist threat (see Ezek. 38:2-4). However in verses 5 and 6, he includes several Muslim nations, the first of which is Persia, modern-day Iran. Here is a lethal combination of international communism and the nations of Islam. They are all predicted to form a large united force that is well-equipped with powerful offensive weaponry (see Ezek. 38:4).

EZEKIEL 38 PORTRAYS ISRAEL
(EZEKIEL 38:11-13)

You will say, "I will go up against a land of unwalled villages; I will go to a peaceful people, who dwell safely, all of them dwelling without walls, and having neither bars nor gates"—to take plunder and to take booty, to stretch out your hand against the waste places that are again inhabited, and against a people gathered from the nations, who have acquired livestock and goods, who dwell in the midst of the land. Sheba, Dedan, the merchants of Tarshish, and all their young lions will say to you, "Have you come to take plunder? Have you gathered your army to take booty, to carry away silver and gold, to take away livestock and goods, to take great plunder?" (Ezekiel 38:11-13 NKJV)

These verses in Ezekiel 38 describe Israel as:

- A people dwelling securely. This is far from current affairs as multiple rocket attacks are launched into Israel almost daily (verse 8).

- A nation at peace in the Middle East. Every nation that surrounds Israel is at present an outright or potential enemy of Israel (verse 8).

- Dwelling without walls. The well-known and most criticized wall in the world no longer divides Berlin, Germany, but now surrounds Jerusalem (verse 11).

- An extremely wealthy nation. The kind of wealth suggested here does not exist in the present State of Israel. The prophet speaks of a nation with "great plunder" for the taking (verse 13). None of these factors are true of modern-day Israel, so the impending war could not be the one described in Ezekiel 38 and 39.

I believe that Ezekiel 38 and 39 clearly refer to a nuclear-equipped Russian-Iranian led alliance formed to invade Israel in the End Times. Although scholars are divided as to the other nations in the alliance, they tend to agree that no explicit reference is made to the Palestinians, Syrians, Lebanese, Jordanians, or Saudi Arabians all of which have been the most observable opponents of Israel since its inception as a nation. Is the reason why they are not included in the alliance the fact that they will have already suffered a massive defeat before the formation of the Ezekiel 38 alliance from which they have not recovered?

The Pathway to the Kingdom— Repentance and Conversion

Repent therefore and be converted, that your sins may be blotted out, so that times of refreshing may come from the presence of the Lord, and that He may send Jesus Christ, who was preached to you before, whom heaven must receive until the times of restoration of all things, which God has spoken by the mouth of all His holy prophets since the world began (Acts 3:19-21 NKJV).

The pathway to the Kingdom for both Israel and the Church is through repentance and conversion. Israel will be transformed into a people with a Messianic mission. The Church of that time period will be one upon which the Holy Spirit has been poured out afresh. It will be divorced from its humanistic and religious traditions inherited in the Middle Ages and will be newly anointed with a tremendous supernatural dimension of authority and power. Israel will flourish with abundance because the former and latter rains will be poured on it.

ENDNOTES

1. "Muslims in Europe"; http://news.bbc.co.uk/2/hi/europe/4385768.stm; accessed December 21, 2009.
2. "U.S. Army Psychiatrist Held After 13 Killed on Base"; http://www.bloomberg.com/apps/news?pid=20601087&sid=aG3rk2qUfmM4&pos=8; accessed December 21, 2009.
3. The Hadith are anecdotes about Muhammad and other founders of Islam. They are considered important source material about religious practice, law, and historical traditions.

Chapter Five

COMMON DENOMINATORS

In so many ways the Bible is a unique and rather complex book written by some 40 different authors over a period of several hundred years. But there are many common denominators throughout which link the various books together to form a great unified library. To use a common analogy, it is like a giant jigsaw puzzle with hundreds of assorted pieces that, when sorted and put in their proper places, form one great picture depicting human history from creation to its finale. Common themes can be traced from Genesis to Revelation. The Bible is a book of history and prophecy describing the past and predicting the future. By studying all the various parts of the books to closely compare one with another, humankind's history can be traced and the future discerned.

There are also many common denominators that show that various parts of the Bible are describing the same event often seen from different perspectives. The most basic examples of this may be seen in the synoptic Gospels in which Matthew, Mark, and Luke narrate the story of Christ's life, death, and resurrection, each from their unique perspective. Even from a superficial reading of these authors, it is easy to conclude that they are all describing the same subject and events. To gain this impression, it is necessary to compare the various descriptions and make note of the common denominators—similar events and happenings that are referred to by each author. When each of the authors describe specific events in detail, it is easy to see that they are all referring to the same occasion. This principle is surely true of Bible prophets. If the identical issues are mentioned by each writer, is it not reasonable to assume that they are all speaking of the same prophetic event occurring at the same prophetic time frame?

The prophetic paradigm that tells the story of this soon-coming conflict and its ultimate inevitable results is contained mainly in three chapters in the Bible, although various other Scriptures describe the ultimate destruction of several nations allied to the attacks on Israel. These passages are Psalm 83, Joel 3, and Zechariah 12. The descriptions of future events in the Last Days are so similar that they have to refer to the same event. These chapters graphically predict what will ultimately transpire with regard to this specific conflict. The result will dramatically transform the present global situation giving Israel a period of peace, prosperity, and international influence.

I believe this is particularly true regarding the prophecies of Psalm 83, Joel 2, and Zechariah 12. There are certain things mentioned in each of these Scripture passages that are common to all three prophecies. In addition I feel a sense of connectivity between the scenes, and I have a feeling of joyful anticipation on behalf of Israel and her future in the purposes of God. Too many Christian theologians have replaced Israel with the Church and consigned Israel solely to the severity of the Great Tribulation. Although I will agree that Israel will ultimately experience the Tribulation, it will not be an entirely negative experience but rather a challenging and triumphant one when Messianic Israel, as symbolized by the 144,000 of Revelation 7, together with the innumerable company of Gentiles from all nations, kindreds, peoples, and tongues, will be a mighty, reaping army bringing multitudes to the Messiah and His Kingdom. This Tribulation company, who have emerged from the Great Tribulation, have all "washed their robes and made them white in the blood of the Lamb" (Rev. 7:14).

Let's consider some of the common denominators which occur in Psalm 83, Joel 3, and Zechariah 12. There are vital aspects in each of the prophecies that are common to all three of these chapters, thus suggesting that they all relate to the same event.

THE FIRST COMMON LINK IS ISRAEL

"Come," they say, "let us wipe out Israel as a nation. We will destroy the very memory of its existence" (Psalm 83:4).

The one basic concept that binds this alliance together is their common determination to totally eliminate the Jewish State of Israel. The very existence of Israel as a Jewish State is seen as an embarrassing insult to Islam. In some extremists' opinion, the fact that this land and city was once ruled by Islam and is now in the hands of Jewish infidels is a slight that must be rectified. The name Israel inevitably links the land to the God of the Bible. Islamic fundamentalists are determined to sever this link and establish the name of Allah and Islam as supreme over Israel and the world.

> *"At that time, when I restore the prosperity of Judah and Jerusalem," says the LORD, "I will gather the armies of the world into the valley of Jehoshaphat. There I will judge them for harming My people, for scattering My inheritance among the nations, and for dividing up My land"* (Joel 3:1-2).

> *"Then you will know that I, the LORD your God, live in Zion, My holy mountain. Jerusalem will be holy forever and foreign armies will never conquer her again"* (Joel 3:17).

Whenever the word LORD occurs in capital letters in the English text, it is a translation of Yaweh (or Jehovah). So the prophet is saying that Jehovah alone is God and that Zion is His holy mountain forever and will be the place of His eternal abode. By this statement, Jehovah is stating and proclaiming His legitimate legal right to Mount Zion in the city of Jerusalem.

> *I will make **Jerusalem and Judah** [Israel] like an intoxicating drink to all the nearby nations that send their armies to besiege Jerusalem* (Zechariah 12:2).

THE SECOND COMMON LINK IS JERUSALEM

> *"At that time, when I restore the **prosperity of Judah and Jerusalem**," says the LORD, "I will gather the armies of the world into the valley of Jehoshaphat"* (Joel 3:1-2).

"Then you will know that I, the LORD your God, live in Zion, my holy mountain. Jerusalem will be holy forever, and foreign armies will never conquer her again" (Joel 3:17).

*Behold, I will make **Jerusalem** a cup of drunkenness to all the surrounding peoples, when they lay siege against Judah and Jerusalem. And it shall happen in that day that I will make Jerusalem a very heavy stone for all peoples; all who would heave it away will surely be cut in pieces, though all nations of the earth are gathered against it* (Zechariah 12:2-3 NKJV).

THE THIRD LINK—
THE SURROUNDING NATIONS

...They signed a treaty as allies against You these Edomites and Ishmaelites, Moabites and Hagrites, Gebalites, Ammonites, and Amalekites, and people from Philistia and Tyre. Assyria has joined them, too, and is allied with the descendants of Lot (Psalm 83:5-8).

"What do you have against Me, Tyre and Sidon and you cities of Philistia? Are you trying to take revenge on Me? If you are, then watch out! I will strike swiftly and pay you back for everything you have done" (Joel 3:4).

I will make Jerusalem and Judah like an intoxicating drink to all the nearby nations that send their armies to besiege Jerusalem (Zechariah 12:2).

...They [Israel] will burn up all the neighboring nations right and left, while the people living in Jerusalem remain secure (Zechariah 12:6).

THE FOURTH LINK—GAZA AND LEBANON

Gebalites, Ammonites, and Amalekites, and people from Philistia and Tyre (Psalm 83:7).

What do you have against Me, Tyre and Sidon and you cities of Philistia? Are you trying to take revenge on Me? If you are, then watch out! I will strike swiftly and pay you back for everything you have done (Joel 3:4).

It is far from coincidence that the spearhead of the threat against Israel is Gaza and Southern Lebanon. The terrorist groups established in these two regions will continue to wage war on Israel until the conclusion predicted in the Bible transpires. The war that was recently waged over Gaza will erupt again (and again?) until it reaches frightening proportions.

THE FIFTH LINK—FIERCE FIRE

As a fire roars through a forest and as a flame sets mountains ablaze, chase them with your fierce storms; terrify them with your tempests (Psalm 83:14-15).

On that day I will make the clans of Judah like a brazier that sets a woodpile ablaze or like a burning torch among sheaves of grain. They will burn up all the neighboring nations right and left, while the people living in Jerusalem remain secure (Zechariah 12:6).

THE CRITERIA BY WHICH GOD JUDGES THE NATIONS

1. They have scattered His chosen people throughout the earth.
2. They have persecuted and harmed His scattered people.
3. They have divided "His Land"—Israel.

Chapter Six

THE BATTLE PREDICTED
IN PSALM 83

Psalm 83 was written by Asaph who was primarily a musician who wrote much of the music that accompanied King David's poems. However, Asaph was also a prophet. This particular psalm is a prophetic psalm predicting a future war. In Psalm 83 the psalmist describes a threatened attack on Israel by Israel's nearest neighbors that is aimed at "wiping Israel off the map, that her name should be remembered no more." The very nations that will mount this attack are named and shamed in this amazing prophetic psalm.

The war in Gaza against Hamas (December 2008-January 2009) is most certainly a critical event in the rapidly developing biblical apocalyptic scenario. I believe this war is one step closer to the massive confrontation between Israel and all her Muslim neighbors that is predicted in several prophetic scriptures (Psalm 83, Joel 3:1-3, Zechariah 12:1-10, and others) discussed in the previous chapter. A chain of events has been set in motion in Gaza and Lebanon that may never end until a direct personal intervention of the Messiah occurs. Such an intervention may well be the one forecast in Zechariah 12:9-10, when immediately after delivering Israel from a massive attack from surrounding nations, Messiah Yeshua reveals Himself personally and explicitly to the House of Israel. In this incident, all the tribes and clans of Israel and even the land itself goes into mourning and repentance before the previously pierced Messiah. The fact that the people mourn in a traditionally Hebraic manner indicates that they recognize Messiah as an authentic Jew.

Many today don't recognize the significance of the Muslim-inspired war on Israel predicted in Psalm 83 and in other Bible prophecies. This psalm predicts an Arab-Israeli war specifically involving *The tents of Edom and the Ishmaelites; Moab and the Hagrites; Gebal, Ammon, and Amalek; Philistia with the inhabitants of Tyre,* that are contrived to demolish the Jewish State. Most Christian commentators cite the Ezekiel 38 and 39 nations as the next opponents who attack Israel.

The following conclusions about biblical and modern-day regions are the result of my many years of studying the Bible and Bible history. Psalm 83 describes a dramatic conflict between Israel and the surrounding Arab nations that will eventually climax in a fierce attack in which Israel will experience a supernatural victory over the Arab armies. There will be a manifestly divine intervention. Psalm 83 verse 6 gives details about some of these nations. Most Bible scholars agree that although Israel has been under attack from all of these ancient neighbors at some time in her long history, ancient Israel was never actually confronted by this specific alliance of nations, namely, *Ishmaelites, Edom, Ammon, Amalek, Hagarenes, Gebal, and the Philistines.* The modern-day equivalent of these nations are all Muslim neighbors of Israel united only by their common determination to annihilate the Jewish State. Therefore, this prophecy obviously has an end-time fulfillment. These Old Testament territories are currently the nations of Jordan, Lebanon, Iraq, Saudi Arabia, and Syria.

Obviously the *Philistines* represent the Palestinians. *Edom, Moab, and Ammon* occupy what is now the modern state of Jordan. *Gebal* is Lebanon (see Josh. 13:5-6). Iraq was populated by the *Hagarenes* or *Hagarites* who dwelt east of Gilead in the wilderness of the River Euphrates (see 1 Chron. 5:1,9-10). The *Ishmaelites* settled what is today Saudi Arabia. *Ishmael's eldest son,* Nabajoth, is identified with Syria.

Lebanon (Gebal) and *Tyre* play a prominent role in Psalm 83. Hezbollah is headquartered in Tyre, which has been heavily attacked by Israel's army in the current war. Since the recent war launched against Israel from Lebanon, Hezbollah has been re-armed by Iran and is making obvious preparations to launch a further stronger attack on Israel. The sequence of events outlined in Psalm 83 parallel the events described in Zechariah 12, and both prophecies appear to refer to the same war.

The psalmist begins by describing a united conspiracy against Israel (see Ps. 83:1-3). They are united together against the Israelites, their aim is the total annihilation of Israel to possess the land so that the very name Israel will no longer be remembered. Although each of these tribal groups is an historic enemy of Israel and have all attacked her on various occasions, there is no record in the Bible that they have ever previously joined in this particular alliance of nations against Israel. All of the cited nations are currently obsessed with an Islamic-inspired determination to completely eliminate the Jewish State of Israel.

THE EVIL ALLIANCE OF NATIONS

There is a belief that the Roman Empire will be revived in Europe and will finally consist of ten nations of which the ten toes of Daniel's image are symbolic (see Daniel 2:24-45). This alliance would have its headquarters in Rome and will possibly be the European Union. However, the part of the Roman Empire to which Bible prophecy alludes is the eastern portion, which encompasses much of the Middle East.

The capital of this eastern kingdom was Constantinople in Turkey and its rule stretched across the Middle East. It is very interesting and significant that the psalmist mentions these people groups in this prophetic psalm. The Arab Alliance presently consists of 22 member states. Only recently and for the first time in their long history have all the Arab nations agreed on a single issue—the complete destruction of the Jewish State of Israel. The nations where the ten ancient people groups and tribes mentioned in Psalm 83 live today are: Lebanon, Syria, Jordan, Iraq, Saudi Arabia, and the Palestinian territories within Israel.

The predictions are specific and accurate in Psalm 83. And in Psalm 81 there is an interesting passage:

> *Oh, that My people would listen to Me, That Israel would walk in My ways! I would soon subdue their enemies, and turn My hand against their adversaries. **The haters of the LORD would***

pretend submission to Him, but their fate would endure forever (Psalm 81:13-15 NKJV).

Verse 15 speaks of a people who actually hate God (Yaweh) when they think in their mind that they submit to Him. The word Muslims means submitters to God (Allah). Islam literally means "submission." In essence, when one reads Psalm 83:2 (KJV), "For, lo, thine enemies make a tumult: and they that hate thee have lifted up the head" is saying that the enemies in this Psalm (Ishmaelites, Hagrites, Assyrians, Lot, Edom, and the people of Tyre) who think in their minds they submit to God, but in reality are full of religious pride and indeed are defiant haters of the true God.

Notice also that this prophecy is future—at the end of days. So in reality, Psalm 83 has not been fully fulfilled; there is another event that must happen in order for it to be completely fulfilled. The ultimate result will be as revealed in Psalm 83:18 (NKJV):

That they may know that You, whose name alone is the LORD [Jehovah], *are the Most High over all the earth.*

The reason God will cause Israel to be so powerfully victorious is as a witness to the Arabs and Muslims and all pagans. A major part of their future armies will perish, but many will recognize and submit to the God of Israel.

These ancient peoples are forerunners of modern nations that are presently allied against Israel, bent upon her destruction and the eradication of the Jewish State. Each of these nations has expressed their hatred of Israel many times since the formation of the Jewish homeland in 1948. The hatred of Israel by her near neighbors has been expressed for more than 60 years in four major wars and thousands of terrorist attacks using rockets, missiles, and suicide bombers. Terror and hatred attacks continue to escalate with no end in sight.[1]

"Come," they say, "let us wipe out Israel as a nation. We will destroy the very memory of its existence" (Psalm 83:4).

PSALM 83

Psalm 83 is so full of richness, let's take a closer look:

O God, don't sit idly by, silent and inactive! Don't You hear the tumult of Your enemies? Don't You see what Your arrogant enemies are doing? They devise crafty schemes against Your people, laying plans against Your precious ones. "Come," they say, "let us wipe out Israel as a nation. We will destroy the very memory of its existence." This was their unanimous decision. They signed a treaty as allies against You [God]. *These Edomites and Ishmaelites, Moabites and Hagrites, Gebalites, Ammonites, and Amalekites, and people from Philistia and Tyre* [Gaza and Southern Lebanon]. *Assyria has joined them, too, and is allied with the descendants of Lot. Do to them as you did to the Midianites or as you did to Sisera and Jabin at the Kishon River. They were destroyed at Endor, and their decaying corpses fertilized the soil. Let their mighty nobles die as Oreb and Zeeb did. Let all their princes die like Zebah and Zalmunna,* [see Judges 8:21,25] *for they said, "Let us seize for our own use these pasturelands of God!" O my God, blow them away like whirling dust, like chaff before the wind! As a fire roars through a forest and as a flame sets mountains ablaze, chase them with Your fierce storms; terrify them with Your tempests. Utterly disgrace them until they submit to Your name, O LORD. Let them be ashamed and terrified forever. Make them failures in everything they do, until they learn that You alone are called the LORD* [God] *that You alone are the Most High, supreme over all the earth.*

The opening words of Psalm 83 echo a statement made on numerous occasions by the leader of Iran whose nation is supporting and fostering the present hostilities against Israel.

ATTACKING JEHOVAH

The nations that have attacked and will attack Israel are Muslim nations. Muslim forces that attack Israel are actually attacking Jehovah, the God of Israel, in the name and authority of Allah. When the future attack ends in a conclusive victory for Israel, fanatical Muslims will submit and surrender to Jehovah and acknowledge His supreme pre-eminence and proven sovereignty.

Following the conclusive and humiliating defeat, they will solemnly declare, "There is no God but Jehovah, and Yeshua Ha Maschiach is His Son."

Psalm 83:16 calls for all nations to submit to God who *alone is God* supreme over *all* the earth (v. 18). God is the One True God and beside Him there is no other.

Political tension in the Middle East is increasing daily. It is becoming increasingly more obvious that a serious war is ready to erupt in the Middle East and that Israel will be the target against which the war will be launched. Several adjacent nations including Iran, Syria, Iraq, Lebanon, Jordan, and others are obviously preparing even now for a massive attack upon Israel.

In Psalm 83, Asaph laments because he sees great danger ahead for Israel. His country is hemmed in by hostile neighbors' intent on Israel's destruction. He prays that God would destroy them and protect His chosen people as He had in past historic wars. This was a very grave situation; and the psalmist turns immediately to God for help. These surrounding enemy nations are cunningly plotting against God's chosen people. They have no respect for Jehovah and plan to wipe out Israel for the honor of their own pagan god. They want to push the Israeli's into the sea and eradicate any remembrance of them.

Asaph desperately wanted God's wrath to be like a stormy tempest from which Israel's enemies could not escape. He wanted God to set the very mountains on fire to destroy them. He prayed that the wicked enemies that insult God by their hostility, arrogance, and violence would be humiliated and totally disgraced.

Let's take another look at this amazing psalm:

> *Do not keep silent, O God!* [Elohim] *Do not hold Your peace, and do not be still, O God! For behold, Your enemies make a tumult; and those who hate You have lifted up their head* [signifying arrogance and pride] (Psalm 83:1-2).

The enemies mentioned by Asaph are not only enemies of Israel, they are vehement enemies of Jehovah. When addressing God, Asaph says "Your enemies." These enemies are not atheists as the communist nations are. They are religious, and their agenda is a religious one. Their attack is upon the God of the Bible who is, according to His own declaration, "The Holy One of Israel." Although Islam has a place in their theology for Isa (Jesus), they are at odds with almost everything that the Bible teaches about Jesus. They fervently deny His divinity, His death and resurrection, and the fact that His blood has atoned for the sins of humankind. They demean and belittle the role of Christ in the plan of salvation demoting Him to a mere prophet like Moses. In fact it would not be an exaggeration to say that their faith is actually anti-Christ in as much as they are aggressively antagonistic to the whole biblical agenda of Christ and the Kingdom of God.

It will appear initially that God is completely silent, detached, and indifferent to the plans and strategies of the alliance that threatens the destruction of Israel, but His apparent disinterest belies His true intentions. These vicious yet cowardly nations are violent enemies of God. In the New International Version of the Bible, it reads, "See how your enemies are astir [active, busy, frenetic], how your foes raise their heads" [in arrogant defiance] (Ps. 83:2 NIV).

Today's headlines copy the language in Psalm 83; the nations aligned against Israel are Israel's current neighbors. Edom and the Ishmaelites were in the land occupied by southern Jordan today, while the territories of Moab and Ammon make up the rest of that country. (While the government of Jordan presently has a peace treaty with Israel, we should remember that some 70 percent of Jordan's population is composed of Palestinians; and in fact, the country was originally formed to be the Palestinian homeland.)

They have taken crafty counsel against Your people, and consulted together against Your sheltered ones (Psalm 83:3).

Through crafty secretive counsel some Arab nations pretend to want peace, while at the same time recruit and train terrorists. Talk about peace agreements is actually hudnas—a time to recoup and re-arm. Asaph said, "With cunning, they conspire against your people; they plot and make evil plans against those you cherish." An aspect of

Islamic belief and culture that the Western world fails to comprehend is that all lies and deceit are perfectly acceptable if those lies further the ultimate cause of Islam. Fanatical Muslims will lie and misinform without hesitation to further their Islamic cause. It is therefore impossible to reach a true peace agreement because they can relent at any time that best suits their purpose. While Islam seeks to portray itself as a religion of peace, its agenda is actually one of jihad or "holy war," which encourages the death and destruction of all who do not profess allegiance to Allah.

> *They have said, "Come, and let us cut them off from being a nation, that the name of Israel may be remembered no more"* (Psalm 83:4 NKJV).

As an example of their determined intent, Arabic maps used in Palestinian schools now show Palestine, but not the nation of Israel. It is this type of warped reality that keeps Israel from taking their threats lightly. Fanatics fervently believe what they say and they are dedicated to carrying out every evil plan. It is their aim, in preparing the world for the advent of their Mahdi or Messiah, to destabilize the world in every possible manner.

> *For they have consulted together with one consent; They form a confederacy against You* (Psalm 83:5 NKJV).

The Arab Alliance of nations conspire together. The one thing that unites them is their mutual determination to eliminate Israel. Although some Muslim nations pretend to stand aloof from the more radical and fanatical elements in Islam, ultimately when the lines are drawn I believe they will all stand together against those they perceive to be their mutual common enemies.

> *The tents of Edom and the Ishmaelites; Moab and the Hagrites; Gebal, Ammon, and Amalek; Philistia with the inhabitants of Tyre* (Psalm 83:6-7 NKJV).

This consortium of nations includes Palestinians (Philistines), and many citizens of Southern Lebanon (Tyre) who are inspired by terrorist organizations like Hamas and Hezbollah.

Assyria also has joined with them; They have helped the children of Lot (Psalm 83:8 NKJV).

Asaph begs God to deal with them as He did with Midian when they attacked Israel in her historic past.

Deal with them as with Midian, as with Sisera, as with Jabin at the Brook Kishon, who perished at En Dor, who became as refuse on the earth. Make their nobles like Oreb and like Zeeb, yes, all their princes like Zebah and Zalmunna, who said, "Let us take for ourselves the pastures of God for a possession" (Psalm 83:9-12 NKJV).

Asaph, the writer of this Psalm, cannot resist telling the Lord God exactly how he'd like Israel's enemies to be dealt with. He remembers that Midian was defeated by a vastly outnumbered force under the command of Gideon. The Lord God turned Israel's enemies against each other, thus causing them to defeat one another (see Judg. 8). Jabin was a king of the Canaanites and Sisera was the commander of his army. The Lord lured the Canaanite army into a trap, and the Israelites destroyed them (see Judg. 4). Oreb, Zeeb, Zebah, and Zalmunna were all leaders of the Midianite army defeated by Gideon (see Judg. 8).

Let their mighty nobles die as Oreb and Zeeb did. Let all their princes die like Zebah and Zalmunna (Psalm 83:11).

Asaph's prayer is that Israel's current enemies will be just as soundly defeated as were the Midianites and the Canaanites when their armies were scattered and their leaders executed. When this prayer is answered, Israel will become much larger geographically, with the contention over ownership of Gaza, the West Bank, and the Golan Heights brought to an end. Israel will become stronger, not weaker, its military reputation will be restored and enhanced. The divided land will be divided no more, and Jerusalem will remain a unified city. The controversial security fence will come down, since the borders on all sides will be safe and the threat of terrorist attacks eliminated. Sixty years of war will temporarily end. It will be the perfect opportunity for the enemy to bring about a false sense of security and turn Israel into a peaceful and unsuspecting people living in a land of unwalled villages as predicted in Ezekiel 38:11.

> *O my God, make them like the whirling dust, like the chaff before the wind! As the fire burns the woods, and as the flame sets the mountains on fire, so pursue them with Your tempest, And frighten them with Your storm* (Psalm 83:13-15 NKJV).

As surely as Israel's (and God's) enemies are marked for destruction, so sure is the outpouring of salvation and righteousness from Heaven upon all nations that fear God. And in the wake of that comes the revelation of Messiah to Israel.

> **Destruction is certain** *for those who argue with their* [true] *Creator. Does a clay pot ever argue with its maker? Does the clay dispute with the one who shapes it, saying, "Stop, you are doing it wrong!" Does the pot exclaim, "How clumsy can you be!"* (Isaiah 45:9)

I personally believe that just as this prophetic word to Cyrus was amazingly and miraculously fulfilled, so it will be fulfilled again to Israel in her present challenging situation. This time the promised Messiah the Redeemer from Zion, will be her deliverer. He will fulfill all of God's righteous purposes.

God's Enemies Humiliated

> *Fill their faces with shame, that they may seek Your name, O GOD* (Psalm 83:16 NKJV).

Loss of face is a dreadful thing in Arabic culture as in many Asian cultures. It causes chronic fear and dismay. Millions of Muslims will "lose face" and be absolutely humiliated when the forces that represent Islam are overwhelmingly defeated. Loss of face is the root cause of so-called "honor killings." They will have then realized that Allah cannot save them and they will turn to the true and living God. The name that they will begin to call upon is that of Jehovah.

> *Let them be confounded and dismayed forever; yes, let them be put to shame and perish,* [faces filled with shame; let them lose

face], *that they may know that You, whose name alone is God, are the Most High over all the earth* (Psalm 83:17 NKJV).

The resounding victory that Jehovah will gain at the conclusion of the war we are discussing will produce worldwide reverence and awe of Jehovah, the God of the Holy Bible and the Holy One of Israel. The implications of that name that inextricably connects Jehovah to Israel eternally, will become clear for all the nations to see. The immediate result of this victory will be a completely changed attitude toward Almighty God, which will precipitate a vast and glorious spiritual harvest. There will be an intense awareness of the awesome authority of Jehovah and His righteousness which will produce an atmosphere of conviction, repentance, and the desire of men to possess the righteousness, joy, and peace that are intrinsic to the universal atmosphere of earth under Jehovah's rule.

However, there will also be pockets of resistance and strong resentment against the followers of the Messiah, both Jew and Gentile. Much of this will be directed against Israel and her people, but it will also be manifest in a fierce persecution of all the worshipers of God. God will provide special protection and covering for His people who will bear His mark.

Paul reminds us that if Israel's temporary rejection made possible the acceptance and inclusion by God of all Gentiles and the restoration of Israel to God's plan, it will be nothing short of a glorious resurrection from the dead.

> *For since their rejection meant that God offered salvation to the rest of the world, their acceptance will be even more wonderful. It will be life for those who were dead!* (Romans 11:15)

PAUL IMPLORES THE CHURCH

For I do not desire, brethren, that you should be ignorant of this mystery, lest you should be wise in your own opinion, that blindness in part has happened to Israel until the fullness of the Gentiles has come in. And so all Israel will be saved, as it is written: "The Deliverer will come out of Zion, and He will turn away ungodliness from Jacob; for this is My covenant with them, when I take away their sins" (Romans 11:25-27 NKJV).

In too many Christian circles there is a deliberate suppression of Israel's vital and indispensable importance in the events of the End Times. Almost all references to Israel are relegated to the Millennium period, and the Church appropriates all the positive promises that occur before that time.

ENDNOTE

1. Israel Science and Technology, "Arab-Israeli Conflict: Basic Facts"; http://www.science.co.il/Arab-Israeli-conflict.asp; accessed January 16, 2010. Rit Nosotro, "The Development of Israel Since 1948," http://www.hyperhistory.net/apwh/essays/cot/t1w30israel48on.htm; accessed January 16, 2010.

Chapter Seven

The Prophecy According to Joel

The prophecy of Joel (circa 795-755 B.C.) is inextricably linked to the war predicted in Psalm 83. Although parts of his prophecy have a fulfillment in the historic past, they also have a definite reference to the Last Days and the prophetic future of Israel, the Church, and humankind.

The Valley of Divine Judgment

For behold, in those days and at that time, when I bring back the captives of Judah and Jerusalem, I will also gather all nations, and bring them down to the Valley of Jehoshaphat; and I will enter into judgment with them there on account of My people, My heritage Israel, Whom they have scattered among the nations; they have also divided up My land (Joel 3:1-2 NKJV).

The Valley of Jehoshaphat means the valley where God judges. In this Scripture passage, the reason He judges the nations at that time will be twofold.

First, because they have scattered God's people among many nations and persecuted and harmed them. Second, because they have sought to divide "God's land."

Many Bible prophecies have the capability of multiple fulfillments and some of the prophecies of Joel fall into this category. His prophecies deal with several phases of world history. One of the most treasured predictions of Joel relates to the promised outpouring of God's Spirit on all flesh. This promise is clearly for the Last Days.

And it shall come to pass afterward that I will pour out My Spirit on all flesh; your sons and your daughters shall prophesy, your old men shall dream dreams, your young men shall see visions. And also on My menservants and on My maidservants I will pour out My Spirit in those days (Joel 2:28-29 NKJV).

However, the context of these verses in Joel 2 reveals a definite connection with what God is performing specifically for Israel. Before the Spirit is poured forth on *all flesh*, it will be poured out upon Israel. Preceding this glorious event though, is a very solemn call to repentance and the sounding forth of a rousing alarm concerning the Day of the Lord, which is then at hand.

Joel 2:28 tells us clearly that, "After I have poured out My rains on Israel" I will pour out My Spirit on *all* flesh. God is going to visit the people of Israel before He pours out His Spirit on *all flesh*. A work of sovereign grace will be enacted upon Israel before God pours out His Spirit on the rest of the world.

Joel's prophecy is extremely pertinent to our present theme. This is especially true for the most part in Joel 3. Our theme is also vitally linked to the latter part of chapter 2 which commences with a call to repentance and a warning of coming calamity. In Joel 2:17, the priests (leaders and ministers of the Lord) are called upon to lead the nation to repentance with weeping and intercession before the God of Israel whose name has been abused and misused by the Gentile heathen who brazenly ask, "Where is the God of Israel?" They intimate that He must be helpless and incapacitated for His authority in Israel appears to be dismally absent.

Let the priests, who minister in the LORD's presence, stand and weep between the entry room to the Temple and the altar. Let them pray, "Spare your people, LORD! Don't let your special possession become an object of mockery. Don't let them become a joke for unbelieving foreigners who say, 'Has the God of Israel left them?'" (Joel 2:17)

THE CHURCH AND ISRAEL
WILL FLOURISH TOGETHER

In the first chapter of Joel both the vine (Church) and the fig tree (Israel) are said to be dry and withered. The inference may be that Israel's tree has been ringbarked by legalism and religious traditions of men. The Church's tree has also been mutilated by replacement theology.

> *The vine has dried up, and the fig tree has withered* (Joel 1:12 NKJV).

However they are both said to be restored and renewed in Joel 2:22 (NKJV), "…The fig tree and the vine [do] yield their strength." Through the spiritual revival that results from urgent prayers and intercessions, Israel and the true Church will become united.

Some years ago when my family and I were living in Africa, God spoke to Elizabeth, my wife, and me. He said, "I want you to get your attitude toward Israel into a right biblical perspective. The effectiveness of your ministry in the future will depend upon you having a right attitude toward Israel and the Jewish people." This book is one result of the steps I have taken to remedy my defective thinking.

I believe His message to me is also an urgent call to *all* God's servants, both Jew and Gentile. It will be an especially powerful moment when Jew and Gentile pray together in unity. The threatened calamity against Jerusalem will produce a call to intercession which will unite true Christian believers with Israel. True Christians will become "Christian Zionists" in the purest biblical sense. In response to such urgent and fervent prayer, God assures Israel that "**I AM**" is among His people Israel and will perform something great on their behalf because of which they will never be disgraced again.

> *Then you will know that **I AM** here among my people of Israel and that I alone am the LORD your God. My people will never again be disgraced like this* (Joel 2:27).

God then promises that in the latter days He will pour out of His Spirit upon all flesh (every nation and people). This is the very promise to which Peter refers on the Day of Pentecost inferring that it was the *beginning* of that which Joel spoke of.

Peter did not infer that what was happening in their ears and before their eyes that day was the complete fulfillment of Joel's prophecy, but that it was the initial stage of what Joel had predicted. Everything that Joel predicted was not fulfilled that day. Joel had predicted that there would be "signs in the heavens, the sun turned to darkness the moon into blood and on the earth would be fire and pillars of smoke." (See Joel 2:30-32.) These signs did not appear on the Day of Pentecost but will be a feature of outpouring in the Last Days.

This particular portion of Scripture has become an important part of the foundation for believing that there will indeed be a tremendous worldwide outpouring of spiritual revival and harvest in the Last Days. However, we must never overlook that this promise is made in the first place to Israel and is associated initially with the physical restoration of His people to their fertile land. Joel envisages a glorious restoration and transformation of Israel that will spill over into the nations. But it will begin with a glorious, gracious work of God's Spirit in the land and among the people of Israel. Those of us who are Gentile believers in the God of Israel will need to recognize, acknowledge, and align ourselves with God's prophetic purposes for Israel if we are to participate effectively in the great End Times revival harvest.

The time period in which the harvest takes place is one marked by unusual and fearful events. Like the period of which Isaiah spoke (see Isa. 60:1), it will be a time of gross darkness throughout the world with all the accompanying paranoia that such conditions will perpetuate. However, in that same period of extremes, God will be working powerfully, responding in grace to all who call on His name. This time of salvation will particularly apply to those "on Mount Zion in Jerusalem" who escape destruction and call on the Mighty God of Israel (Jehovah).

> *But everyone who calls on the name of the LORD will be saved, for some on Mount Zion in Jerusalem will escape, just as the LORD has said. These will be among the survivors whom the LORD has called* (Joel 2:32).

Judgment Against Israel's Enemies

Another portion of Joel's predictions deal with God's judgment of the nations in the valley of Jehoshaphat for their treatment of Israel.

I will gather the armies of the world into the valley of Jehoshaphat. There I will judge them for harming My people, My special possession, for scattering My inheritance among the nations, and for dividing up My land (Joel 3:2).

Since 1948 we have witnessed in part the amazing restoration and prosperity of Israel. Since 1967 we have also witnessed the restoration into Jewish control the city of Jerusalem. The remainder of Joel's prophecy flows in the wake of this restoration. God says, "In that time period" certain specific things will occur. The main sign will be an attack on Jerusalem by her Muslim neighbors with the tacit political support of many other nations. Their persistent call will be for the dividing of Israel and of Jerusalem. This call will purport to be a call for peace, but it will precipitate war which will conclude with a massive victory for Israel.

The warnings in Joel 3:2 apply initially to those nations that have scattered the Jews in the Diaspora over the past 2,000 years and treated them shamefully and painfully. However, they also apply very much to what is happening in Israel now in the 21st century.

On a given day in the future, God will arraign the nations before Him to judge the acidity of their souls. The test will be how they have regarded the Jew and the Jewish nation. Those nations that have been positive, receptive, and kind toward the Jew will be regarded as "sheep nations." In complete contrast, those that have harbored negative attitudes toward them and treated them despicably will be seen as "goat nations." With respect to His Kingdom, God will say to the sheep, "Come, inherit the Kingdom of My Father." But to the goat nations He will say, "Depart from Me!" (see Matt. 25:32-34).

Regarding the stance of many nations toward Israel today, the world is already divided in its attitude, but will soon polarize dramatically. Sadly, I believe that the church too will be dramatically polarized and divided over the most divisive issue it has ever faced—its attitude toward Israel. The Jewish nation of Israel in natural terms is a democratic, capitalist nation that has successfully re-established itself in its ancient homeland after an absence of some 2,000 years. Its main ambition is to provide an egalitarian society for Jewish people most of whom are refugees escaping discrimination and persecution. Its natural growth, development, and achievements, while surrounded by hostile enemy nations, have been nothing short of incredible and highly commendable.

From the tragic Holocaust in Europe and continued anti-Semitic persecution worldwide, the population of Israel, composed of Jewish people from more than 100 nations, has not only become the most successful democracy in the Middle East, it remains the only legitimate democracy in that region. Her sole aim is to provide a haven of safety and security for those who wish to live in the land that God gave them. In complete contrast, the stated purpose and ambition of neighboring nations is to destroy Israel and its population. What does God's litmus test reveal about the hearts of these nations and even about His Church?

LATTER DAYS

I firmly believe that the very existence of Israel today unmistakably places us in the latter days. If this is indeed the case, a correct understanding of the End Times is essential for every believer. The Body of Messiah needs to be prepared for what is about to take place in the world. If the pre-tribulation doctrine proves to be incorrect, then many Christians who were expecting to be raptured at any moment may find themselves totally unprepared to survive severe tribulation. The Lord has called us to be His co-workers. Therefore we need to know what lies before us, so we can invest our lives intelligently and sacrificially in the work of the Kingdom. Let us also remember that Jesus rebuked the people of His day for being able to discern the weather from the signs in the sky, but not able or willing to discern the signs of the prophetic times in which they lived.

He replied, "You know the saying, 'Red sky at night means fair weather tomorrow, red sky in the morning means foul weather all day.' You are good at reading the weather signs in the sky, but you can't read the obvious signs of the times! (Matthew 16:2-3)

Jesus will not take His bride out of this world until she is complete with both Jews and Gentiles. The Jews have been blinded to this truth and have suffered dreadfully for the last 2,000 years, so that you, if you are a Gentile, could be grafted in. That is why Paul also says in Romans 15:27 that it is our duty to bless the Jewish people in every possible way. We are called to be intercessors on the walls of Jerusalem since the day that we came into the Kingdom.

They threw dice to decide which of My people would be their slaves. They traded boys to obtain prostitutes and sold girls for enough wine to get drunk (Joel 3:3).

This verse refers to the manner in which many nations have treated Jewish people despicably because of their beliefs. Many nations at various times have treated Jewish people as worthless beings of less value than the price of a drunken revelry. They have treated Jews as goats rather than sheep and for this, one day, Almighty God will judge severely them.

What do you have against Me, Tyre and Sidon and you cities of Philistia? Are you trying to take revenge on Me? If you are, then watch out! I will strike swiftly and pay you back for everything you have done (Joel 3:4).

Joel speaks about the Palestinians "selling the people of Israel" to the Greeks. I believe that this is a reference to the radical Palestinians who are now eagerly courting the favor of the European nations as part of a plan to remove all Israelis "far from their homeland"— from Israel.

*You have taken my silver and gold and all my precious treasures, and you have carried them off to your pagan temples. You have sold the people of Judah and Jerusalem to the Greeks, who took them **far from their homeland**. But I will bring them back again from all these places to which you sold them, and I will pay you back for all you have done* (Joel 3:5-7).

In Joel 3:4, God specifically addresses two geographic areas that are central to the problems with which Israel has to deal with today— Gaza and Southern Lebanon. How interesting that after all these years these are the two main danger areas confronting Israel. Hamas in Gaza and Hezbollah in Southern Lebanon are two terrorist organizations funded, trained, and equipped by Iran and integrated into a strategy to destroy Israel. They are both fanatically intent on bringing death and destruction upon Israel. But death and destruction will come back on their own heads. What they seek to do to Israel will happen to them. Although this threat may belong originally to a previous era, I believe that it also has a definite link to the present situation in the Middle East. Once again, old enemies are united against Israel—this time in the form of Hezbollah in Tyre and Sidon in Southern Lebanon and Hamas in Philistia (Gaza).

Isaiah 2:4 will only be fulfilled when Christ is enthroned in Jerusalem. Before that time comes, unfortunately, the opposite will happen. God will draw the armies of the world into the Valley of Jehoshaphat ("God Judges"). They will imagine they are marching toward victory over Israel and the conquest of that land, but they will actually be marching toward divine judgment. God will judge them in such a powerful and convincing manner that the whole world will have a healthy fear of Him. A sense of reverent awe will fill the hearts of multitudes. Millions will surrender to the proven Lord of the universe.

> *Let the nations be called to arms. Let them march to the valley of Jehoshaphat. There I, the LORD, will sit to pronounce judgment on them all. Now let the sickle do its work, for the harvest is ripe. Come, tread the winepress because it is full. The storage vats are overflowing with the wickedness of these people* (Joel 3:12-13).

The harvest of the ages will dawn. Divine judgment will come upon the wicked and rebellious, and righteousness upon the repentant.

> *Thousands upon thousands are waiting in the valley of decision. It is there that the day of the LORD will soon arrive* (Joel 3:14).

The Hebrew word for decision comes from a root word for uncertainty, insecurity, or consternation, implying severe anxiety, alarm, and dismay. It portrays a time of darkness and fear among all nations. It sounds very much like what Jesus spoke of in Luke 21:25-28.

The prophet Joel says, "**The LORD's voice will roar** from Zion and thunder from Jerusalem, and the heavens and the earth will shake. But the LORD will be a refuge for his people, a strong fortress for the people of Israel" (Joel 3:16).

Please also note that God's voice will thunder *from Zion and Jerusalem.* At this time His presence will be situated specifically in that place—Mount Zion and Jerusalem. He declares this to be His "dwelling place" and that foreign armies will never conquer Jerusalem again.

Throughout history God has pardoned Israel many times for repeated infringements of His Law. However, Joel 3:21 intimates that at this future date He will clear the books of all her "crimes" and make His home in Jerusalem with His people.

The World's Greatest Harvest

Within the Church and its community there are numerous extremely varied and disparate views as to whether this present era will conclude with a great harvest/revival or an appalling apostasy. My firm belief is that both of these views are true. There will be a powerful and glorious harvest, but there will also be a great apostasy. One's response to Israel and the God of Israel will make the difference as to whether you experience one or the other. This tremendous harvest of souls into God's Kingdom will happen first in Israel and then in the nations. (See Joel 2:18-19, 23-24, 28-29.)

This tremendous worldwide harvest will begin after God judges the nations that attack Israel and try by every means first to divide and then to conquer His land (see Joel 3:1-2). This treacherous action against Jehovah and His people will bring upon the heads of Israel's enemies a momentous and miraculous defeat, after which God will pour out His Spirit upon Israel and the inhabitants of Jerusalem.

WHEN WILL THESE THINGS HAPPEN?

As mentioned previously, some Christian commentators have relegated Israel's exaltation and glorification to the Millennium. They have also consigned Israel to the Great Tribulation while the Church, having been raptured, is enjoying the Marriage Supper of the Lamb. They also believe that since Israel apparently rejected Jesus as the Jewish Messiah, God has irrevocably replaced them with the Church. However, Paul points out that it is the gifts and callings of God which are truly irrevocable (see Rom. 11:29).

> *And so all Israel will be saved, as it is written: "The Deliverer will come out of Zion, And He will turn away ungodliness from Jacob; for this is My covenant with them, When I take away their sins." Concerning the gospel they are enemies for your sake, but concerning the election they are beloved for the sake of the fathers. For the gifts and the calling of God are irrevocable* (Romans 11:26-29 NKJV).

Irrevocable means binding, final, irreversible, unalterable, permanent, immutable, and unchallengeable. Such is the status and standing of Israel before God. His promises to them have never been altered, withdrawn, rescinded, or made obsolete. He is eternally The Holy One of Israel.

Chapter Eight

TOMORROW'S HEADLINES
IN ZECHARIAH

The war in Gaza which broke out in December 2008 will explode again until finally it will be launched in such a fashion that with Iranian support it will threaten Israel as a Jewish nation and all Jews and Christians in the land. It will be waged with the threat of weapons of mass destruction. Although the attack will be launched by "all the nearby nations" (Zech. 12:2), it will be politically, financially, and morally supported by many other nations that supply weapons and technical intelligence. This war will precede by some years the Ezekiel 38 and 39 war which will be waged years after a peace treaty with Israel has given them a period of peace and prosperity.

The prophet Zechariah predicted that in the Last Days all the nations surrounding Jerusalem would launch a fierce attack upon Israel and Jerusalem. These nations would be complicit in one purpose—the elimination of the State of Israel. However, the prophet saw that instead of eliminating Israel, the God of Israel will destroy and eradicate them. God will also preserve Israel and the citizens of Jerusalem. The prediction in Zechariah is all the more remarkable when we realize that it was pronounced approximately 2,600 years ago.

The twelfth chapter of Zechariah is among the most important chapters in the Bible. It is a chapter of prophetic predictions that will usher Israel into the most exciting and fulfilling days of her entire history. It will introduce Israel into the fullest expression of her predicted role as a holy nation and a kingdom of priests. Israel will inherit her predicted function as a Messianic nation that will proclaim the Kingdom reign of God over all nations.

SEQUENCE OF EVENTS

The sequence of events that we will track in this chapter is as follows:

1. An attack upon Israel by all her surrounding neighbors.

2. The conclusive supernatural defeat inflicted by God upon Israel's anti-God enemies (see Zech. 12:2-9).

3. God's miraculous defense of Israel and Jerusalem.

4. The confidence that Israel's leaders will express. "Then the leaders of Judah will think to themselves, 'The people who live in Jerusalem are strong because of the LORD of Armies, their God'" (Zech. 12:5).

5. The conclusive victory of God's army over the armies of Islam.

6. The submission of Muslims to the demonstrated superiority of Jehovah.

7. The outpouring of the Holy Spirit upon Israel and the inhabitants of Jerusalem (see Zech. 12:10).

8. The prayers, mourning, and repentance of Israel regarding their deliverer the Messiah and their submission to Him.

9. The Messianic transformation of Israel.

10. The manifestation of the One New Man.

11. A tremendous worldwide harvest of souls into the Kingdom.

ZECHARIAH 12:1—FUTURE DELIVERANCE FOR JERUSALEM

This message concerning the fate of Israel came from the LORD: "This message is from the LORD, who stretched out the heavens, laid the foundations of the earth, and formed the spirit within humans" (Zechariah 12:1).

Zechariah emphasizes the fact that Jehovah is the unique Creator of the heavens, earth, and all humankind. He is the one true and living

God, Creator and Ruler of the universe. He is the omnipotent God for whom nothing is impossible, and He will come to the aid of Israel when all hope of survival seems to have disappeared. Isaiah also speaks of the creative omnipotence of God, emphasising His ability to accomplish anything and everything.

Although the initiative for this battle appears to come from the attacking armies, it actually comes from God Himself who draws them into a confrontation in order to judge them for their sins against His people Israel.

The scenario that follows, reveals the absolute sovereignty of God as He vents His anger and judgment for recurrent historic mistreatment of His people and also for their final attempt to divide the land that He has promised them. All the nations that are part of the plot to divide the Promised Land will suffer some measure of judgment; but those that actually launch this attack, will suffer the most.

> *I will make Jerusalem and Judah like an intoxicating drink to all the nearby nations that send their armies to besiege Jerusalem* (Zechariah 12:2).

God will give the enemies of Israel an intoxicating cup that will cause fearful trembling. The attacking armies will begin to behave irrationally like a drunken mob. Their clarity of purpose and coordination will suffer grievously. God will also sow madness (insanity) and confusion through the ranks of Israel's enemies. In the Bible, such a cup in the hands of God usually speaks of a cup of judgment and obviously such is the case in this chapter. God will force the enemies of Israel to drink from His intoxicating cup of judgment.

> **On that day** I will make Jerusalem an immovable rock. All the nations will gather against it to try to move it, but they will only **hurt themselves** (Zechariah 12:3).

The heavy stone will rupture everyone who tries to move it. The picture is of a human being endeavoring to move a gigantic rock or boulder much larger than oneself and succeeding only in rupturing himself.

The phrase "On that day," which is used consistently in this chapter of Zechariah, is often called "The Day of the Lord" and suggests a particular time frame in the last days. According to Nelson's dictionary, the Day of the Lord is, "A special day at the end of time when God's will and purpose for mankind and His world will be fulfilled. Many Bible students believe the Day of the Lord will be a long period of time rather than a single day, a period when Christ will reign throughout the world before He cleanses heaven and earth in preparation for the eternal state of all mankind. But others believe the Day of the Lord will be an instantaneous event when Christ will return to earth to claim His faithful believers while consigning unbelievers to eternal damnation."[1]

MUCH TO SAY ABOUT "THAT DAY"

That Day is a euphemistic term for the period at the close of this age. It is referred to by several different names and is rather loose in its interpretation. It is often called The Day of Messiah by Jewish people.

That Day is a special period at the end of time when God's will and purpose for humankind and His world will be fulfilled. The phrase appears 17 times in Zechariah 12–14, giving consistency and connection to all the events therein. The reference connects and builds all the events of these chapters toward the crescendo and finale of the book.

> *In that day "HOLINESS TO THE LORD" shall be engraved on the bells of the horses. The pots in the LORD's house shall be like the bowls before the altar. Yes, every pot in Jerusalem and Judah shall be holiness to the LORD of hosts...* (Zechariah 14:20-21 NKJV).

The governors and citizens of Israel will confess that Jehovah Sabaoth is their living God and that their true strength is in Him. By the power of God, the leaders of Israel in that day will come to trust and rely upon the Lord Almighty. This title is a military name that means the "Lord of Armies." It confirms the fact that God is going to assume a genuine military role in behalf of Israel at this time.

And the governors of Judah shall say in their heart, "The inhabitants of Jerusalem are my strength in the LORD of hosts, their God" (Zechariah 12:5 NKJV).

The clans (tribes) of Israel will become like a prairie fire in a forest of dry timber or a torch thrown among dry sheaves of wheat. Israel's counter attack against the invaders will be like an immense explosion of a fiery tempest destroying all the attacking enemy armies.

On that day I will make the clans of Judah like a brazier that sets a woodpile ablaze or like a burning torch among sheaves of grain. They will burn up all the neighboring nations right and left, while the people living in Jerusalem remain secure. The LORD will give victory to the rest of Judah first, before Jerusalem, so that the people of Jerusalem and the royal line of David will not have greater honor than the rest of Judah (Zechariah 12:6-7).

The nation of Israel will receive deliverance first before Jerusalem. The attack will evidently be initiated in the territory outside of Jerusalem.

On that day the LORD will defend the people of Jerusalem; the weakest among them will be as mighty as King David! And the royal descendants will be like God, like the angel of the LORD who goes before them! (Zechariah 12:8)

THE ANGEL OF THE LORD

The word translated weakest or feeblest is *kabal* which suggests "one that totters or wavers through inadequate strength particularly in the legs." This can refer to tiny infants or elderly persons. He further emphasizes that the Angel of the Lord, the Messiah, will actually lead Israel into battle. In typical Israeli Defense Force fashion, He will go before His troops as the Supreme Commander. He will be wholly responsible for their amazing strategy.

Headline news in all forms of international media will one day carry the story, "**Israel Wins Astonishing Victory Through Supernatural**

Intervention!" The accompanying articles will retell the amazing prophetic fulfillment of a war originally foretold in Zechariah:

> *In that day the LORD will defend the inhabitants of Jerusalem; the one who is feeble among them in that day shall be like David, and the house of David shall be like God, like the Angel of the LORD before them* (Zechariah 12:8 NKJV).

The Angel of the Lord mentioned in verse 8 is none other than the Messiah. The code name *Angel of the Lord* is used numerous times in the Old Testament for visible appearances and physical manifestations of God.

The Angel of the Lord is a mysterious messenger of God, sometimes described as the Lord Himself (see Gen. 16:10-13; Exod. 3:2-6; 23:20; Judg. 6:11-18), but at other times as one sent by God. The Lord used this messenger to appear to human beings who otherwise would not be able to see Him and live (see Exod. 33:20).

Zechariah 12:8 tells us that Messiah was the One who went before them into battle and won for them a tremendous, supernatural victory. In the aftermath of this amazing battle, when the tide is suddenly and supernaturally turned in Israel's favor, a bewildered Israel will look around to see who has achieved this supernatural victory on their behalf. It is then that they will suddenly recognize their Deliverer as Yeshua HaMashiach whose hands were pierced through crucifixion, and they will mourn over Him in great bitterness of soul.

> *Then I will pour out a spirit of grace and prayer on the family of David and on all the people of Jerusalem. They will look on Me whom they have pierced and mourn for Him as for an only son. They will grieve bitterly for Him as for a firstborn son who has died* (Zechariah 12:10).

This appearance of the Messiah is not the Rapture nor the Second Coming. Rather, it is a unique intimate private appearance of the Messiah to Israel at which time their national spiritual blindness will be sovereignly healed. They will finally recognize that Yeshua is their promised Messiah who is actually God who clothed Himself in the likeness of human flesh to redeem humankind. This event will usher in a period of Messianic recognition by Israel that will accompany the period of peace and expansion that is the result of the victory of Psalm 83:15-17 and Zechariah 12:9.

Immediately following this great victory, God will pour out His Spirit (Ruach Ha Kodesh) on Israel and Jerusalem. The grace of God will provoke prayers of repentance that will bring the nation into a new living relationship with God. The living relationship of their forefathers whom God brought forth from Egypt will be resurrected and will explode into a spiritually renewed and completely restored people.

What makes the time element of this scenario so imminently threatening is that Iran, who is presently fighting this war by proxy, will have soon produced enough enriched uranium to manufacture a nuclear arsenal.[2] Of course Iran claims that her nuclear program is only for electrical energy for civilian use. However, Iran already has the missiles to deliver nuclear warheads.[3] Hundreds of Russian scientists in Iran are helping to develop long range missiles.[4]

For My plan is to destroy all the nations that come against Jerusalem (Zechariah 12:9).

God has determined to destroy all the nations that align themselves against Jerusalem whether in person or by proxy. Initially for the immediately surrounding nations, this will mean resounding defeat; but those nations that do not physically enjoin the battle but give political and philosophical support to that strategy will suffer judgment too.

Zechariah 12:10 is one of the most remarkable verses in the Bible. To me it is obvious that the LORD (Jehovah) is speaking and He says, "They shall look on **Me** whom they have pierced." This clearly suggests that Yeshua, the pierced One (see John 19:34,37 and Rev. 1:7), is actually God manifested as the second person of the trinity.

THE SECOND PERSON OF THE TRINITY

The amazing truth that God was actually pierced is supported in the New Testament. It was not the Jews who crucified Him. It was the Romans, and it was our own sins that nailed Him to the cross. (See 2 Corinthians 5:19.)

Some Christian commentators have suggested that John 19:37 is the fulfillment of Zechariah 12:10. In suggesting this they willfully ignore the very plain end-time context of the chapter. Another Christian commentator suggests that the commander-in-chief of the Israeli army was fatally pierced in battle plunging the nation into grief and mourning.

John Gill's Exposition says: "We Christians can have no doubt that this passage belongs to Christ, when it is observed, upon one of the soldiers piercing the side of Jesus with a spear, it is said, 'these things were done that the Scripture should be fulfilled; they shall look on him whom they have pierced.'"

Numerous other commentators make similar observations without any apparent reference to the very obvious immediate context of Zechariah 12:10, which clearly ascribes the prophecy of Zechariah to the last days and not the first advent of Jesus. These commentators assume that the prophecy was fulfilled at Calvary when those who crucified Jesus, "looked on Him whom they had pierced." However, the reference in Zechariah obviously refers to a future prophetic occasion when, after a major attack on Israel and an amazing victorious intervention led by the Messiah, Israel will then gaze on Him who once was crucified as the Lamb of God and now returns as the Deliverer from Zion.

As mentioned previously, many churchmen throughout the centuries, through the introduction of human and often pagan religious traditions, have successfully separated the Church from its original Hebraic roots. However, God has determined to rectify this error by re-grafting Israel's branches back onto their own tree (see Rom. 11:23). Christians should remember that from Israel has come every blessing and privilege that we enjoy.

In my opinion it is unwise to ignore the clear and copious eschatological context of the verse and to deliver a verdict that is plainly at odds with the context. It is plainly stated that the Messiah who is the One who once was pierced, has returned again to Israel as their nation's Deliverer to confront them with the undeniable proof that He is their long-awaited Jewish Messiah.

Zechariah 12:10 is also a remarkable verse in that it says that God's grace will be poured out on the family of David *and on* all the inhabitants of Jerusalem. The population of Jerusalem is presently comprised of Jews, Christians, and Muslims; therefore, this indicates that God's grace and supplications will be poured out upon each of these population groups.

ISRAEL'S DELIVERER

All Israel will suddenly identify their Deliverer as their promised Messiah and grieve bitterly, recognizing Him as the firstborn Son of God. In doing so, Israel will recognize and acknowledge His deity, His redeeming death and resurrection. This revelation will transform the nation of Israel into a people from every tribe of Israel who recognize that the Yeshua HaMashiach is actually God. This whole experience of amazing miraculous deliverance from their enemies through the intervention of Messiah Yeshua and the subsequent pouring out upon them of God's Spirit in grace and supplications, will transform them into a powerful body of Messianic witnesses.

Zechariah 12:8 tells us that the Person they look upon is the One who went before them into battle and won for them a tremendous, supernatural victory. When that battle is concluded, the people of Israel look around in astonishment to discover how that victory was achieved and by whom. Their eyes will look on the Messiah who was once pierced, and they will recognize Him as the promised Messiah of Israel (see Isa. 53).

I believe that a scene in Genesis was a prophetic picture of this end-time event. I am referring to the time when Joseph revealed himself to his brothers. Initially Joseph's brothers did not recognize who he was, but he always knew who they were. So it has been for Israel throughout history. They have not recognized the true identity of Jesus, but He has always recognized them as His brethren after the flesh.

So Joseph recognized his brothers, but they did not recognize him (Genesis 42:8 NKJV).

Joseph could stand it no longer. "Out, all of you!" he cried out to his attendants. He wanted to be alone with his brothers when he told them who he was. Then he broke down and wept aloud. His sobs could be heard throughout the palace, and the news was quickly carried to Pharaoh's palace. "I am Joseph!" he said to his brothers. "Is my father still alive?" But his brothers were speechless! They were stunned to realize that Joseph was standing there in front of them. "Come over here," he said. So they came closer. And he said again, "I am Joseph, your brother whom you sold into Egypt. But don't be angry with yourselves that you did this to me, for God did it. He sent me here ahead of you to preserve your lives. These two years of famine will grow to seven, during which there will be neither plowing nor harvest. God has sent me here to keep you and your families alive so that you will become a great nation (Genesis 45:1-7).

This scene prophetically portrays a closed, intimate meeting between Messiah and His immediate family. All Egyptians (Gentiles) were excluded from the room. The Israelites will immediately recognize exactly who their Deliverer is by the scars in His hands and side, they will recognize Him "whom they pierced."

Notice in Genesis 45:2 that the news of Joseph's unveiling before his brethren was "quickly carried to Pharaoh's palace." So also when Messiah reveals His true identity to Israel, the news will quickly go around the world. The whole nation will grieve and mourn for Him in a typically and traditionally Hebraic manner, and they will be transformed by the revelation. I believe that this leads on to the formation of the one new people of whom Paul spoke (see Eph. 2:15), as Gentile believers take a positive stand together with their Messianic brothers and sisters. Their combined witness will be further augmented by a multitude of the sons of Ishmael and people from every tribe, tongue, and nation (see Rev. 12:1-12, 13:7).

THE LAND GOD PROMISED TO ABRAHAM'S DESCENDANTS

Israel's promised boundaries, which include the Golan Heights, Gaza, and the West Bank, were anciently foretold in Scripture (see Gen. 15:18-21; Micah 7:14; Zephaniah. 2:7; Zechariah 10:9-10).

The territories that God mentions include the very areas that are currently occupied by Israel's former and now present enemies as enumerated in Psalm 83. They are territories that God will cause Israel to inherit once again when He acts as a Shepherd to His people.

> *O LORD, protect your people with your shepherd's staff; lead your flock, your special possession. Though they live alone in a thicket on the heights of Mount Carmel, let them graze in the fertile pastures of Bashan and Gilead as they did long ago* (Micah 7:14).

Isaiah reiterates God's threats against the pagan religions and their devotees,

> *The idols of Babylon, Bel and Nebo, are being hauled away on ox carts. But look! The beasts are staggering under the weight! Both the idols and the ones carrying them are bowed down. The gods cannot protect the people, and the people cannot protect the gods. They go off into captivity together. "Listen to me, all you who are left in Israel. I created you and have cared for you since before you were born. I will be your God throughout your lifetime— until your hair is white with age. I made you, and I will care for you. I will carry you along and save you* (Isaiah 46:1-4).

FALSE GODS DIMINISHED

In the wake of this astonishing victory which God will inflict on the enemies of Israel, the gods of the earth will be shown to be false. Their apparent power will be reduced to nothing, their devotees and followers completely disillusioned. Their influence on millions of devotees will be eliminated and huge numbers of them will acknowledge Jehovah and His Son Yeshua.

The Hebrew prophets Jeremiah and Zephaniah declared approximately 2,600 years ago that their God would some day destroy "all the gods of the earth." Let's look at how these gods surrender their power.

This they shall have for their pride, Because they have reproached and made arrogant threats against the people of the LORD of hosts. **The LORD will be awesome to them, For He will reduce to nothing all the gods of the earth;** *People shall worship Him, (Jehovah) Each one from his place, Indeed all the shores of the nations* (Zephaniah 2:10-11 NKJV).

But the LORD [Jehovah] is the true God; He is the living God and the everlasting King. At His wrath the earth will tremble, and the nations will not be able to endure His indignation. **Thus you shall say to them: "The gods that have not made the heavens and the earth shall perish from the earth and from under these heavens."** *He has made the earth by His power, He has established the world by His wisdom, and has stretched out the heavens at His discretion* (Jeremiah 10:10-12 NKJV).

The point the prophet makes is that his God is far greater than all false gods. In ancient times, a god was said to bless his worshipers in battle, and "greatness" was awarded to the god of the victor. The gods of Zephaniah's prophecy were Chemosh and Milcom. These gods, along with numerous others, were abandoned prior to, or forfeited later, in favor of Allah. By the time the 7th century rolled around, Allah presided as the undisputed god of these Psalm 83 Arab populations. Hence, in accordance with historical Hebrew precedence, comes the understanding that in bitter defeat this god will have failed to deliver his greatness to the Arabs.

Truly, O God of Israel, our Savior, You work in strange and mysterious ways. All who make idols will be humiliated and disgraced. But the LORD will save the people of Israel with eternal salvation. They will never again be humiliated and disgraced throughout everlasting ages. For the LORD is God, and He created the heavens and earth and put everything in place. He made the world to be lived in, not to be a place of empty chaos. "I am the LORD," He says, "and there is no other. I publicly proclaim bold promises. I do not whisper obscurities in some dark corner so no one can understand what I mean. And I did not tell the people of Israel to ask Me for something I did not plan to give. I, the LORD, speak only what is true and right" (Isaiah 45:15-19).

Having dispensed His judgment on Israel's neighboring enemies decisively defeating and humiliating them, God now offers amnesty and peace to the survivors of those same nations. He defeats their leaders and their armies but offers peace to their citizens (see Isa. 45:20-25).

The Israeli-Arab conflict will ultimately culminate in an amazing victory for Israel. The prayer of Psalm 83 will be answered by the Lord. Israel will take back any land previously surrendered including Gaza. Additionally, she will acquire parts of Lebanon, Syria, and Jordan. (See Isaiah 11:14; Zephaniah 2:3-10; Zechariah 10:10.)

"The house of Jacob shall be a fire, and the house of Joseph a flame; but the house of Esau shall be stubble; they shall kindle them and devour them, and no survivor shall remain of the house of Esau," for the LORD has spoken. The South shall possess the mountains of Esau, and the Lowland shall possess Philistia. They shall possess the fields of Ephraim and the fields of Samaria. Benjamin shall possess Gilead. And the captives of this host of the children of Israel shall possess the land of the Canaanites as far as Zarephath. The captives of Jerusalem who are in Sepharad shall possess the cities of the South. Then saviors shall come to Mount Zion to judge the mountains of Esau, and the kingdom shall be the LORD's (Obadiah 1:18-21 NKJV).

This threat has been building up for many years now, in fact ever since the first few days following the official announcement of modern Israel's statehood in 1948. Actually, the original roots originate many centuries before, to the days of Isaac and Ishmael. Finally there will be a temporary cessation of war against Israel and a glorious worldwide harvest of souls will occur.

All Israel and the inhabitants of Jerusalem will acknowledge Yeshua's true Jewish identity and mourn over Him in an authentic Hebraic manner. From this national repentance and recognition of the Messiah will come the new Messianic identity of Israel.

This will be for Israel as life from the dead. "For if their being cast away is the reconciling of the world, what will their acceptance be but life from the dead?" (Romans 11:15 NKJV).

ISRAEL WILL BE SEALED BY GOD

Then I saw another angel ascending from the east, having the seal of the living God. And he cried with a loud voice to the four angels to whom it was granted to harm the earth and the sea, saying, "Do not harm the earth, the sea, or the trees till we have sealed the servants of our God on their foreheads." And I heard the number of those who were sealed. One hundred and forty-four thousand of all the tribes of the children of Israel were sealed (Revelation 7:2-4 NKJV).

These "Israeli" servants of God will be sealed with a special seal in their foreheads. This may or may not be a seal visible to all. It may be a special consciousness of God in their minds. They will obviously herald the message of the Kingdom and their Messiah King.

The number 144,000 is not mathematically precise, but rather symbolic. It will represent the completeness of Israel as per 12x12 tribes. Twelve is also the number of divine government. These servants of God will be marked or sealed by Him.

I believe they will minister in cooperation with the innumerable company that John evidently saw some small distance from them. This is a vast Gentile (non-Jewish) company so large that it cannot be visually estimated. There will be a sublime unity and cohesion between the two groups as they work together in the same glorious cause.

After these things I looked, and behold, a great multitude which no one could number, of all nations, tribes, peoples, and tongues, standing before the throne and before the Lamb, clothed with white robes, with palm branches in their hands, and crying out with a loud voice, saying, "Salvation belongs to our God who sits on the throne, and to the Lamb!" (Revelation 7:9-10 NKJV).

THE HARVEST

- Will be comprised of a great number that no one can estimate.
- Will include people of all nations, peoples, tribes, and tongues.
- Will include people of every religion on earth, Islam, Hinduism, Buddhism, etc.
- Will proclaim in a loud voice the salvation of Jehovah.
- Robes are washed white in the blood of the Lamb.
- Are in willing submission to the rule of Jehovah.
- Are protected from hunger, thirst, and sunstroke forever.
- Will be led by the Lamb to living fountains of water.
- Will be the greatest spiritual harvest ever.

SUGGESTED PROPHETIC TIMELINE

1. This present time period—ends with the Battle for Jerusalem (Ps. 83, Zech. 12)
2. Holy Spirit upon Israel—(Zech. 12:10)
3. Israel's transformation—(Isa. 60, Isa. 24:33, 52:2, 58:8, etc.)
4. Gog and Magog war—(Ezek. 38, 39)
5. Great Tribulation—(Rev. 7:14, etc.)
6. Armageddon—(Rev. 16:16; 20:1-10)
7. Millennium—(Rev. 19:1-16, 20:1-9)

ISRAEL GRAFTED IN AGAIN

As we have seen in Isaiah 66:8, the new Israel will be born in a day. This indicates an instantaneous birth, not a gradual transformation. Isaiah further states that once the process begins, God will not delay delivery or shut up the womb causing a stillbirth.

> *"Who has heard such a thing? Who has seen such things? Shall the earth be made to give birth in one day? Or shall a nation be born at once? For as soon as Zion was in labor, she gave birth to*

her children. Shall I bring to the time of birth, and not cause delivery?" says the LORD. "Shall I who cause delivery shut up the womb?" says your God (Isaiah 66:8-9).

He also clearly indicates that this amazing birth process has to do with Jerusalem. "All who love Jerusalem will exceedingly rejoice with her."

Rejoice with Jerusalem, and be glad with her, all you who love her... (Isaiah 66:10 NKJV).

The apostle Paul says, "And they also, if they **do not continue in unbelief**, will be grafted in, for God is able to graft them in again. For if you [Gentiles] were cut out of the olive tree which is wild by nature, and were grafted contrary to nature into a cultivated olive tree, how much more will these [Jews], who are natural branches, be grafted into their own olive tree? For I do not desire, brethren, that you should be ignorant of this mystery, lest you should be wise in your own opinion, that blindness in part has happened to Israel until the fullness of the Gentiles has come in. And so all Israel will be saved, as it is written: 'The Deliverer will come out of Zion, and He will turn away ungodliness from Jacob; for this is My covenant with them, when I take away their sins'" (Rom. 11:23-27 NKJV).

According to Paul, it will happen when they *"do not continue in unbelief."* In other words, when living faith is instantly quickened into the soul of the nation, Israel will be regrafted into her own olive tree. What kind of circumstance might cause an instantaneous national rebirth of faith? Surely an amazing, miraculous rescue and reprieve from certain annihilation would qualify! When the nation is supernaturally delivered from a very real ominous threat of total extinction and the people, turning to see how this great deliverance was achieved, look directly upon their promised Messiah. Surely this epic moment could achieve instantaneous national faith!

Within the context of this amazing birth process Paul declares, "And so **all** Israel will be saved" (Rom. 11:26). Paul also indicates that all this will happen "when the fullness of the Gentiles has come in." This statement has usually been interpreted to mean when the last of the Gentiles has come into God's family. It has usually been given a missionary context of world evangelism. However, I believe it to mean that the fullness of the Gentiles will be attained when the Jewish branches are regrafted back onto their own olive tree. At that precise time, the One New Man will be formed (see Eph. 2:15).

The apostle Paul speaks of a Deliverer coming from Zion to Mount Zion. In Romans 11:26 he says that the Deliverer will come *from* Zion.

> *In this way Israel as a whole will be saved, as Scripture says, "The Savior will come from Zion. He will remove godlessness from Jacob"* (Romans 11:26 GNT).

But he is actually quoting Isaiah 59:20, which says *to* Zion: "'Then a Savior will come **to Zion**, to those in Jacob who turn from rebellion,' declares the LORD" (GNT).

The grammatical structure and inference of Paul's words suggest that the Savior/Deliverer will come from (heavenly) Zion to (earthly) Zion to turn Israel from their rebellion. The psalmist says that Israel will rejoice when the Deliverer comes from Zion to restore the fortunes of His people Israel.

> *If only salvation for Israel would come from Zion! When the LORD restores the fortunes of His people, Jacob will rejoice. Israel will be glad* (Psalm 14:7 GNT).

ENDNOTES

1. "The Day of the Lord," *Nelson's Illustrated Bible Dictionary*, (Nashville, TN: Thomas Nelson Publishers, 1986).

2. "Iran Vows Not to Suspend Uranium Enrichment"; http://www.msnbc.msn.com/id/17358752/; accessed December 22, 2009.

3. Luke Harding, guardian.co.uk, "Russia will supply new anti-aircraft missiles for Iran," 12/27/07; http://www.guardian.co.uk/world/2007/dec/27/russia.iran; accessed January 16, 2010. Andrew Osborn, telegraph.co.uk, "Arctic Sea was carrying missiles to Iran," 9/11/09; http://

www.telegraph.co.uk/news/worldnews/europe/rus-
sia/6170926/Arctic-Sea-was-carrying-missiles-to-Iran-
new-report-suggests.html; accessed January 16, 2010.

4. Ariel Cohen, "Are Russian Scientists Aiding Iran's Nuclear Program?"; http://corner.nationalreview.com/post/
?q=NDMzNzhiN2IzNGFmYjkxNmY0YjlmN2ViMzc
4ZDJhZWI=; accessed December 22, 2009.

Chapter Nine

DESTRUCTION IN THE MIDDLE EAST

The prayer for deliverance and victory for Israel in the face of her near neighbors' attack is made to God by Asaph in Psalm 83, but the ultimate answer to that fervent prayer is recorded in numerous other parts of the Bible as well, including Zephaniah, Jeremiah, and Obadiah.

The prophet Obadiah says, "The house of Jacob [the Jews] shall be a fire, and the house of Joseph [Jews] a flame; but the house of Esau shall be stubble. They [the Jews] shall kindle and devour them and no survivor shall remain in the house of Esau. For the word of the Lord has spoken (Obad. 1:18).

THE DESTRUCTION OF GAZA

Universal political pressure forced Israel to evacuate the Gaza Strip. That region, adjacent to Israel, has become a hotbed of terrorism through agencies dedicated to Israel's destruction. Israel is under constant threat from terrorists in Gaza. But the Bible gives a severe warning of the repercussions of such terrorism.

For Gaza shall be forsaken, and Ashkelon made desolate; They shall drive out Ashdod at noonday, and Ekron shall be uprooted. Woe to the inhabitants of the seacoast, the nation of the Cherethites! The word of the LORD is against you, O Canaan, land of the Philistines: "I will destroy you; so there shall be no inhabitant." The seacoast shall be pastures, with shelters for shepherds and folds for flocks. The coast shall be for the remnant of the house of Judah; they shall feed their flocks there; in the houses of Ashkelon they shall lie down at evening. For the LORD their God will intervene for them, and return their captives. "I have heard the reproach of Moab, and the insults of the people of Ammon, with which they have reproached My people, and made arrogant threats against their borders. Therefore, as I live," says the LORD of hosts, the God of Israel, "Surely Moab shall be like Sodom, and the people of Ammon like Gomorrah— Overrun with weeds and saltpits, and a perpetual desolation. The residue of My people shall plunder them, And the remnant of My people shall possess them." This they shall have for their pride, because they have reproached and made arrogant threats against the people of the LORD of hosts. The LORD God will be awesome to them, for He will reduce to nothing all the gods of the earth; people shall worship Him, Each one from his place, indeed all the shores of the nations. "You Ethiopians also, you shall be slain by My sword." And He will stretch out His hand against the north, destroy Assyria, and make Nineveh a desolation, as dry as the wilderness (Zephaniah 2:4-13 NKJV).

"Do not rejoice, all you of Philistia, because the rod that struck you is broken; for out of the serpent's roots will come forth a viper, and its offspring will be a fiery flying serpent. The firstborn of the poor will feed, and the needy will lie down in safety; I will kill your roots with famine, and it will slay your remnant. Wail, O gate! Cry, O city! All you of Philistia are dissolved; for smoke will come from the north, and no one will be alone in his appointed times." What will they answer the messengers of the nation? That the LORD has founded Zion, and the poor of His people shall take refuge in it (Isaiah 14:29-32 NKJV).

GOD'S ANGER AGAINST ASSYRIA

God's anger against Assyria (modern-day Iran, Syria and Iraq) is vividly shown in the following passage from Isaiah 14:

The LORD of hosts has sworn, saying, "Surely, as I have thought, so it shall come to pass, and as I have purposed, so it shall stand: that I will break the Assyrian in My land, and on My mountains tread him underfoot. Then his yoke shall be removed from them, and his burden removed from their shoulders. This is the purpose that is purposed against the whole earth, and this is the hand that is stretched out over all the nations. For the LORD of hosts has purposed, and who will annul it? His hand is stretched out, and who will turn it back?"(Isaiah 14:24-27 NKJV)

Obadiah the prophet predicted a time when Israel will "possess" many areas of land currently in the hands of their enemies.

The South shall possess the mountains of Esau and the lowland shall possess Philistia [Gaza strip]. *They shall possess the fields of Ephraim and the fields of Samaria* [West Bank]. *And the captives of this host of the children of Israel shall possess the land of the Canaanites as far as Zarephaph. The captives of Jerusalem who are in Sepharad shall possess the cities of the South* (Obadiah 1:19-20).

THE MIGHTY ONE OF ISRAEL

Isaiah declares the word of God concerning His enemies and their fate. He makes the announcement in the name of Jehovah Sabaoth (Lord of Armies) and El Gibbor (Mighty One of Israel). The raw might and power of God will be demonstrated openly when He awesomely destroys all the enemies of Israel.

Therefore the Lord says, The LORD of hosts, the Mighty One of Israel, "Ah, I will rid Myself of My adversaries, and take vengeance on My enemies. I will turn My hand against you, and thoroughly purge away your dross, and take away all your alloy. I will restore your judges as at the first, and your counselors as at the beginning. Afterward you shall be called the city of righteousness, the faithful city." Zion shall be redeemed with justice, and her penitents with righteousness. The destruction of transgressors and of sinners shall be together, and those who forsake the LORD shall be consumed (Isaiah 1:24-28 NKJV).

Jeremiah takes up a similar cry: "At that time I will bring to the throne of David a righteous descendant, and he will do what is just and right throughout the land. **In that day Judah will be saved, and Jerusalem will live in safety. And their motto will be 'The LORD is** our righteousness!' For this is what the LORD says: David will for-ever have a descendant sitting on the throne of Israel" (Jer. 33:15-17).

GOD'S ROADMAP TO PEACE

God's plan calls for the Palestinians to resettle in the lands of their ancestry. He promises a fertile future to those Arabs who obediently adhere to His command. His roadmap clearly requires that the Palestinians and their Arab cohorts support Israel, and turn their affections toward Jehovah, Jeremiah's God. If they fail to do all of this, then a severe reprisal will be levied for their national disobedience:

> *But any nation who refuses to obey Me* [Jeremiah's God] *will be **uprooted and destroyed**. I, the LORD* [God], *have spoken!* (Jeremiah 12:17).

CONCLUSIONS

The following conclusions can be drawn from the Word of God:

1. The Psalm 83 nations will form an alliance against Israel in non-compliance with God's roadmap plan.
2. United States and United Nations Middle East peace efforts will fail to prevent an Arab-Israeli war.
3. The Arab States that attack Israel are destined for divine judgment.
4. Israeli Defense Forces will shock the world with a show of superior strength.
5. The Jewish State will expand its sovereignty over cap-tured Arab soil.
6. The world will witness Israel become one of its wealthi-est nations.
7. Peace in the Middle East will be achieved militarily rather than politically or diplomatically.

Opposition to Israel is a fundamental principle in Shi'ite Muslim Iran, which backs Palestinian militants opposed to peace talks.

In 2008, Iran's President Mahmoud Ahmadinejad made vitriolic statements pronouncing the death of Israel and America before the full council of the United Nations in New York without drawing much adverse comment or criticism.[1] He has consistently reiterated his violent remarks to a worldwide audience, making clear his unwavering intention to annihilate Israel. President Ahmadinejad said that Israel was "dying" and that people in the Middle East would soon destroy it when given the chance.

According to a May 14, 2008, Reuters.uk article, during Israel's 60th anniversary celebrations, Ahmadinejad said, "The Zionist regime is dying." He further said in a speech referring to Israel, "The criminals imagine that by holding celebrations…they can save the Zionist regime from death. They should know that regional nations hate this fake and criminal regime and if the smallest and briefest chance is given to regional nations they will destroy [it]."[2]

In 2005 Ahmadinejad said that "Israel should be wiped off the map" and that Israel would "be soon swept away" by the Palestinians. A senior Iranian army commander said Iran would respond to an Israeli attack by "eliminating" Israel.[3]

Consider these excerpts from a sermon delivered live over Palestinian television October 13, 2000, by Dr. Ahmad Abu Halabiya: "…the Jews must be butchered and killed, as Allah the almighty has said." "Wherever you meet them, kill them (and kill those Americans who are like them and who stand by them.)"[4]

The Ayatollah Khomeini of Iran stated that the primary purpose of the Iranian Republic is to take back the land of Palestine for Allah, exterminating Israel in the process.[5]

Osama bin Laden has also echoed these sentiments but in addition he urged Jihad (holy war) against Americans. He said, "The ruling to kill the Americans and their allies—civilians and military—is an individual duty for every Muslim who can do it in any country in which it is possible to do it, in order to liberate the al-Aqsa Mosque and the holy mosque from their grip, and in order for their armies to move out of all the lands of Islam, defeated and unable to threaten any Muslim. This is in accordance with the words of Almighty

Allah, 'and fight the pagans all together as they fight you all together,' and "fight them until there is no more tumult or oppression, and there prevail justice and faith in Allah."[6]

Most Christians know the verses that predict that every knee will one day bow before the Lord:

> For it is written: "As I live, says the LORD, every knee shall bow to Me, and every tongue shall confess to God" (Romans 14:11 NKJV).

> Therefore God also has highly exalted Him [Jesus] and given Him the name which is above every name, that at the name of Jesus every knee should bow, of those in heaven, and of those on earth, and of those under the earth, and that every tongue should confess that Jesus Christ is Lord, to the glory of God the Father (Philippians 2:9-11 NKJV).

However, few Christians connect every knee bowing with the following Scripture passage in Isaiah:

> I have sworn by Myself; the word has gone out of My mouth in righteousness, and shall not return, that to Me every knee shall bow, every tongue shall take an oath. He shall say, "Surely in the LORD I have righteousness and strength. To Him men shall come, and all shall be ashamed who are incensed against Him. In the LORD all the descendants of Israel shall be justified, and shall glory" (Isaiah 45:23-25 NKJV).

This is the original "every knee will bow verse" yet some never study the immediate context. Look at the next sentence that follows: "Bel boweth down, Nebo stoopeth, their idols were upon the beasts and upon the cattle" (Isa. 46:1 KJV).

What was on the beasts and cattle? There were crescent moons upon the animals—this is now the internationally recognized symbols of Islam. These same symbols will bow before God (see Judges 8). Turkey and many other Muslim nations include a crescent moon symbol on their national flag and emblems. Muslim country and mosques fly the crescent at the highest points for all to see.

THE BATTLE CRY

Messiah is compared to Gideon who is an intriguing and interesting character; he represents the War Messiah. This story is documented in Judges 8: "...So Gideon arose and killed Zebah and Zalmunna, and took the crescent ornaments that were on their camels' necks" (Judg. 8:21 NKJV).

It is a generally held view that Allah is a pre-Islamic name corresponding to the Babylonian god known as Bel. Allah is the moon god of Babylonia—Bel. This symbol will bow. In other words, all minarets with crescents on top will be taken down—to bow. Mystery Babylon (see Rev. 17:5) is *not* Rome as popularly thought or the Catholic Church, but it is instead Islam and Arabia.

The Muslim's battle cry in every battle, victory, or demonstration is "Allah Akbar" which means: "Allah is Greatest." Greater than who? Greater than any god, but especially Jehovah, the God of the Jews and the Christians. So what is the essence of Psalm 83? It is verse 18, which declares "that men may know that only God's name is the Most High."

The power of Islam is permeating throughout the world, but the power of God will soon be manifested in a dramatic and powerful manner that will overthrow many Muslim nations.

Islamic theology vehemently denies the attributes, purposes, and supremacy of Jehovah, the God of the Bible. The main thesis of Islamic doctrine is the claim that the Bible of the Jews and Christians is a distorted and discredited document. It strongly refutes the claim that Jehovah is the one true and living God above all other gods and that Jesus Christ is the Son of God. Islam is insidiously endeavoring to destroy the credibility of Judaism and Christianity and fill the earth with its message that Allah is supreme. However, the power of Jehovah will soon be manifested in such a powerful and convincing manner that the whole world will recognize that Jehovah alone is the one true and living God.

Several prophetic passages predict the destruction of Damascus in the Last Days. Damascus is presently the home base for many terrorist organizations obsessed with bringing down Israel. Could it be that when they finally go too far and Israel retaliates, the result may well be the destruction of Damascus?

ISAIAH 17:1-3—A PROCLAMATION AGAINST SYRIA

"Behold, Damascus will cease from being a city, and it will be a ruinous heap. The cities of Aroer are forsaken; they will be for flocks which lie down, and no one will make them afraid. The fortress also will cease from Ephraim, The kingdom from Damascus, and the remnant of Syria; They will be as the glory of the children of Israel," says the LORD of hosts (NKJV).

JEREMIAH 49:24-27—A PROPHECY AGAINST DAMASCUS

Damascus has grown feeble; she turns to flee, and fear has seized her. Anguish and sorrows have taken her like a woman in labor. Why is the city of praise not deserted, the city of My joy? Therefore her young men shall fall in her streets, and all the men of war shall be cut off in that day," says the LORD of hosts. "I will kindle a fire in the wall of Damascus, and it shall consume the palaces of Ben-Hadad" (NKJV).

Thus says the LORD: "For three transgressions of Damascus, and for four, I will not turn away its punishment, because they have threshed Gilead [Jezreel Valley] *with implements of iron. But I will send a fire into the house of Hazael, Which shall devour the palaces of Ben-Hadad. I will also break the gates of Damascus, and cut off the inhabitant from the Valley of Aven, and the one who holds the sceptre from Beth Eden. The people of Syria shall go captive to Kir, says the LORD* (Amos 1:3-8).

THE PREDICTED DESTRUCTION OF GAZA

The LORD says, "The people of Gaza have sinned again and again, and for this I will certainly punish them. They carried off a whole nation and sold them as slaves to the people of Edom.

So I will send fire upon the city walls of Gaza and burn down its fortresses. I will remove the rulers of the cities of Ashdod and Ashkelon. I will punish the city of Ekron, and all the Philistines who are left will die" (Amos 1:6-8 GNT).

Zechariah 9 has an extremely interesting word concerning Syria, Lebanon, and Gaza:

The burden of the word of the LORD against the land of Hadrach, and Damascus its resting place (For the eyes of men and all the tribes of Israel are on the LORD); also against Hamath, which borders on it, **and against Tyre and Sidon,** *though they are very wise. For Tyre built herself a tower, heaped up silver like the dust, and gold like the mire of the streets. Behold, the LORD will cast her out; He will destroy her power in the sea, and she will be devoured by fire.* **Ashkelon shall see it and fear; Gaza also shall be very sorrowful;** *and Ekron, for He dried up her expectation. The king shall perish from Gaza, and Ashkelon shall not be inhabited. "A mixed race shall settle in Ashdod, and I will cut off the pride of the Philistines. I will take away the blood from his mouth, and the abominations from between his teeth. But he who remains, even he shall be for our God, and shall be like a leader in Judah, and Ekron like a Jebusite"* (Zechariah 9:1-7 NKJV).

Does any of this seem plausible? Is it possible that these threats to annihilate Israel will be intentionally launched in the very near future? You can follow the daily news and see Bible prophecy unfold! The exact details of all that will transpire are not known. I am simply presenting you with certain prophecies that give a strong indication that many current and future events constitute their fulfillment.

It appears that Israel may now be very close to this war in fulfillment of this and numerous other prophecies. In conjunction with these prophecies, there are a number of other Scriptures that provide details of the extent of the territorial gains that Israel may achieve in the next war.

Biblical predictions for the outcome of this war are abundant. Prophecies such as Ezekiel 36, Isaiah 16–17, Psalm 83, Psalm 60–61,

Ezekiel 25:15-17, Jeremiah 49:23-27, and Zechariah 9 and 12, are samplings of the preview that God has provided about this imminent war. Psalm 83:9-12 describes an overwhelming victory on a scale superseding the devastating battles from Bible times.

War against Damascus is described in detail in Jeremiah: "Against Damascus. 'Hamath and Arpad are shamed, for they have heard bad news. They are fainthearted; There is trouble on the sea; It cannot be quiet. Damascus has grown feeble; She turns to flee, And fear has seized her. Anguish and sorrows have taken her like a woman in labor'" (Jer. 49:23-24 NKJV). And "Therefore her young men shall fall in her streets, And all the men of war shall be cut off in that day," says the LORD of hosts. "I will kindle a fire in the wall of Damascus, and it shall consume the palaces of Ben-Hadad" (Jer. 49:26-27 NKJV).

EZEKIEL DESCRIBES PALESTINE'S DESTRUCTION

In most versions of the Bible there are very few actual references to "Palestine" but in each one of those that do occur there are warnings of severe judgment to come upon Palestine. (Philistia is the ancient name for Palestine.)

Thus says the Lord GOD: "Because the Philistines dealt vengefully and took vengeance with a spiteful heart, to destroy because of the old hatred," therefore thus says the Lord GOD: "I will stretch out My hand against the Philistines, and I will cut off the Cherethites and destroy the remnant of the seacoast. I will execute great vengeance on them with furious rebukes; and they shall know that I am the LORD, when I lay My vengeance upon them" (Ezekiel 25:15-17 NKJV). Note: Cherethites are an ancient tribe of Philistines who emigrated from Crete to Israel.

Indeed, what have you to do with Me, O Tyre and Sidon, and all the coasts of Philistia? Will you retaliate against Me? But if you retaliate against Me, swiftly and speedily I will return your retaliation upon your own head (Joel 3:4 NKJV).

"Do not rejoice, all you of Philistia, Because the rod that struck you is broken; for out of the serpent's roots will come forth a viper, and its offspring will be a fiery flying serpent. The firstborn of the poor will feed, and the needy will lie down in safety; I will kill your roots with famine, and it will slay your remnant. Wail, O gate! Cry, O city! All you of Philistia are dissolved; for smoke will come from the north, and no one will be alone in his appointed times." What will they answer the messengers of the nation? That the LORD has founded Zion, and the poor of His people shall take refuge in it (Isaiah 14:29-32 NKJV).

Ashkelon shall see it and fear; Gaza also shall be very sorrowful; and Ekron, for He dried up her expectation. The king shall perish from Gaza, and Ashkelon shall not be inhabited (Zechariah 9:5 NKJV).

We made an invasion of the southern area of the Cherethites, in the territory which belongs to Judah, and of the southern area of Caleb; and we burned Ziklag with fire (1 Samuel 30:14 NKJV).

Then at last the people [nations] will think of their Creator and have respect for the Holy One of Israel (Isaiah 17:7).

...for the eyes of all humanity, especially the people of Israel, are on the LORD (Zechariah 9:1).

The worldwide End-Times outbreak of hatred toward the Jewish people may be the impetus for another great wave of aliyah (immigration), the final mass movement of the majority of Jewish people still in Diaspora back to the land God promised them. Zechariah foresaw this also. He supplied us with incredible details about this final aliyah that fit beautifully with this scenario. In the vision the Lord gave Zechariah, he saw that those returning to the land would be returning not only to what constitutes Israel's current boundaries, but also to portions of western Jordan and southern Lebanon. For this to happen, Israel will capture this land in the war.

I will signal for them and gather them in. Surely I will redeem them; they will be as numerous as before. Though I scatter them among the peoples, yet in distant lands they will remember Me. They and their children will survive, and they will return. I will bring them back from Egypt and gather them from Assyria. I will bring them to Gilead and Lebanon, and there will not be room enough for them (Zechariah 10:8-10 NIV).

The glory of Lebanon will be yours—the forests of cypress, fir, and pine—to beautify My sanctuary. My Temple will be glorious! (Isaiah 60:13)

No matter how unlikely this may seem to most observers now, it will certainly happen. God has declared these things, and they will surely come to pass. Everything He has predicted will happen just as He promised.

What are God's intentions in all of this? It is all about Israel's spiritual awakening, for His glory. The well-known prophecy in Isaiah 60 does not initially apply to the Church, but to Israel. It predicts that the glory of God will arise over Israel, and the Gentiles including the nearby (Muslim) nations of Midian, Ephah, Sheba, Kedar, and Nebaioth will come to her light. (See Isaiah 60:1-7.)

ISRAEL'S EXCEEDINGLY GREAT ARMY

So I prophesied as He commanded me, and breath came into them, and they lived, and stood upon their feet, an exceedingly great army (Ezekiel 37:10 NKJV).

In Ezekiel's prophecy, God predicts the return of Israel to their land and within that land the raising up of an exceedingly great army. Since 1948, that army has come into being. It is not exceedingly great numerically, but it is certainly great in its effectiveness and achievements. Numerous armies boasting far greater numbers have been humbled and defeated by Israel's army, but in the forthcoming war with her Arab neighbors, the Israel Defense Force (under God's great hand) will win its greatest victory ever! God's intervention on Israel's behalf is going to be more conspicuous and dramatic than ever before.

GOD'S JUDGMENT

God's judgment on those who despise Israel will be swift and complete.

> *"And there shall no longer be a pricking brier or a painful thorn for the house of Israel from among all who are around them, who despise them. Then they shall know that I am the Lord GOD." Thus says the Lord GOD: "When I have gathered the house of Israel from the peoples among whom they are scattered, and am hallowed in them in the sight of the Gentiles, then they will dwell in their own land which I gave to My servant Jacob"* (Ezekiel 28: 24-25 NKJV).

KINGDOMS RISE AND FALL

An amazing fact of history is that numerous once-mighty kingdoms have all fallen and disintegrated because of their negative treatment of the Jewish people. The latest such kingdom is the powerful and far-reaching British Empire. It was said of this family of nations that, "the sun never sets on the British Empire." But shortly after World War II, when Britain reneged on her promise to Israel, the empire rapidly fell apart. God's curse falls on all whom satan inspires to despise the Jews/Israel, and it has a global dimension. History shows kingdoms rise and fall according to how they relate to Israel because, "Thus says YHWH of hosts, after the glory has He sent Me unto the nations which spoiled you [Zion]: for he that touches you touches the apple of His eye" (Zech. 2:8; cp. Deut. 32:10).

In Jeremiah 30:12-15, God says that Israel deserves punishment for her sin. However, immediately after that, He warns those who dare touch her, declaring, "all that devour you shall be devoured; ...They that spoil you shall be a spoil, and all that prey upon you will I give for a prey" (Jer. 30:16; cp. Jer. 2:3).

THE EDOMITES—OFFSPRING OF ESAU

Ezekiel names many nations who are judged because of how they have dealt with Israel: the Ammonites celebrated Israel's misfortune (see Jer. 25:1-7).

Edom, the descendants of Esau, is an evil spiritual root of Islam. Esau, also known as Edom, was the eldest son of Jacob and legally entitled to inherit Jacob's blessing. Unfortunately for Esau he did not value his privileged birthright and in fact despised it and sold it for a bowl of red soup for which action his name became Edom (Red).

> And Esau said to Jacob, "Please feed me with that same red stew, for I am weary." Therefore his name was called Edom (Genesis 25:30 NKJV).

> And Esau said, "Look, I am about to die; so what is this birthright to me?" Then Jacob said, "Swear to me as of this day." So he swore to him, and sold his birthright to Jacob. And Jacob gave Esau bread and stew of lentils; then he ate and drank, arose, and went his way. Thus Esau despised his birthright (Genesis 25:32-34 NKJV).

Esau later regretted his impetuous action and wept over his foolish behavior.

> And Esau said to his father, "Have you only one blessing, my father? Bless me—me also, O my father!" And Esau lifted up his voice and wept (Genesis 27:38 NKJV).

The bitterness of Esau turned to anger, and he determined to kill his brother Jacob. That bitter determination has continued on through the long line of Esau's descendants manifesting itself in acts of violent terrorism. It remains the root cause of the great hatred of Israel that resides in the hearts of Esau's offspring to this present day.

> So Esau hated Jacob because of the blessing with which his father blessed him, and Esau said in his heart, "The days of mourning for my father are at hand; **then I will kill my brother Jacob**" (Genesis 27:41 NKJV).

The Edomites were the first tribe to seek to deny the children of Israel access to Canaan.

> Then Edom said to him, "You shall not pass through my land, lest I come out against you with the sword." So the children of Israel said to him, "We will go by the Highway, and if I or my livestock

drink any of your water, then I will pay for it; let me only pass through on foot, nothing more." Then he said, "You shall not pass through." So Edom came out against them with many men and with a strong hand. Thus Edom refused to give Israel passage through his territory; so Israel turned away from him (Numbers 20:18-21 NKJV).

The Edomites historically and periodically attacked and fought against the Israelites. They were a continuing thorn in the flesh to Israel.

For again the Edomites had come, attacked Judah, and carried away captives (2 Chronicles 28:17 NKJV).

In Exodus 15, Moses sang a song of prophetic praise to God and called on Him to strike fear into the heart of Edom giving Israel victory over them and entrance into the Promised Land.

Then the chiefs of Edom will be dismayed; The mighty men of Moab, Trembling will take hold of them; All the inhabitants of Canaan will melt away (Exodus 15:15 NKJV).

Modern descendants of Esau still harbor deep resentment against the offspring of Jacob (Israel) and are seeking to deny them their right to the Promised Land. Their hatred is expressed through acts of violent terrorism.

God has threatened Edom with ultimate destruction because of their vicious actions against Israel. He will also judge all who have the spirit of Esau (Edom) in their hearts.

Thus says the Lord GOD concerning Edom (We have heard a report from the LORD, and a messenger has been sent among the nations, saying, "Arise, and let us rise up against her for battle"): "Behold, I will make you small among the nations; you shall be greatly despised" (Obadiah 1:1-2 NKJV).

God has sent a message among the nations to fight against Edom, and to ultimately destroy Edom. Since the days of Esau (Edom) and Jacob (Israel), there has been a constant rivalry between the two. At times they seem to be friendly toward one another, but the vast majority of times Edom is a huge stumbling block to Israel. Since Israel's initial entry into Canaan, they have met with opposition. But God has a message for both Edom and Israel, Edom will be utterly despised not only among Israelites, but among all the nations, and all the nations will rise up against Edom.

> *"Because of what Edom did against the house of Judah by taking vengeance, and has greatly offended by avenging itself on them," therefore thus says the Lord GOD: "I will also stretch out My hand against Edom, cut off man and beast from it, and make it desolate from Teman; Dedan shall fall by the sword. I will lay My vengeance on Edom by the hand of My people Israel, that they may do in Edom according to My anger and according to My fury; and they shall know My vengeance," says the Lord GOD* (Jeremiah 25:12-14 NKJV).

God also threatened to judge Egypt because she was an unfaithful ally to Israel (see Ezek. 29:3-7). This should make all of Israel's modern so-called friends shake with fearful dread. God says that speaking against *His* mountains, the mountains of Israel (Judea and Samaria with Jerusalem in the middle) is blasphemy (see Ezek. 35:10-13). Nations that call this area where the Jews live the "occupied territories," are blaspheming, bringing themselves into the Valley of Jehoshaphat (see Joel 3:1-2), the place of God's righteous judgment.

God says that when He restores all of Israel to her land, they shall dwell there with confidence, **when I have executed judgments upon all those that despise** [curse] **them** round about them; and they shall know I am LORD their God (Ezek. 28:25-26). So God's judgments on Israel's enemies are linked with Israel's spiritual salvation (see Rom. 11:26; cp. Zech. 12:9 with 12:10).

ISRAEL WILL DWELL SECURELY

And they shall dwell safely therein, and shall build houses, and plant vineyards; yea, they shall dwell with confidence, when I have executed judgments upon all those that despise them round about them; and they shall know that I am the LORD their God (Ezekiel 28:26 KJV).

The Jewish State is greatly despised, hated, and abhorred in the eyes of her near neighbors. There is a common bond between those neighbors and it is their united desire to see Israel obliterated. This attitude is clearly reflected in the various biblical passages that support the objective of "wiping Israel off the map" and destroying the very memory of its existence (see Ps. 83:4). But God will never allow that to happen. When those enemies once again attack Israel, they will finally experience God's anger and vengeance against them in a devastating manner.

God's promise that Israel will live safely in her Promised Land is the assurance of a loving God who takes care of His children. This promise is for all those who choose to believe in His unconditional love and redemptive grace and mercy.

ENDNOTES

1. "Ahmadinejad: American Empire Nearing its End"; http://www.cnn.com/2008/WORLD/meast/09/23/ahmadinejad.us/index.html; accessed December 23, 2009.

2. "Iran's Ahmadinejad Says Israel 'Dying'"; http://uk.reuters.com/article/idUKHOS43245220080514; accessed December 23, 2009.

3. Ibid.

4. http://www.aish.com/jw/me/48882612.html; accessed December 23, 2009.

5. "Iranian Leader: Wipe Out Israel"; http://edition.cnn.com/2005/WORLD/meast/10/26/ahmadinejad/; accessed December 23, 2009.

6. Frontline: Hunting bin Laden; http://www.pbs.org/wgbh/pages/frontline/shows/binladen/who/edicts.html; accessed January 16, 2010.

Chapter Ten

ISRAEL WILL REGAIN HER TERRITORIES

One outstanding result of the war between Israel and her neighboring nations will be that Israel will acquire much more land and territory than she has previously held in this modern age. Most of this land is currently in Arab hands. Several Scriptures confirm this.

> *The South shall possess the mountains of Esau. And the lowland shall possess Philistia. They shall possess the fields of Ephraim and the fields of Samaria. Benjamin will possess Gilead. And the captives of **this host of the children of Israel shall possess the land of the Canaanites as far as Zarephaph.** The captives of Jerusalem who are in Sepharad shall possess the cities of the South* (Obadiah 1:19-20 NKJV).

> *"Therefore behold, the days are coming," says the LORD, "That I will cause to be heard an alarm of war In Rabbah of the Ammonites; it shall be a desolate mound, and her villages shall be burned with fire. **Then Israel shall take possession of his inheritance,"** says the LORD"* (Jeremiah 49:2 NKJV).

> *"Therefore, as I live," says the LORD of hosts, the God of Israel, "Surely Moab shall be like Sodom, and the people of Ammon like Gomorrah—overrun with weeds and saltpits, and a perpetual desolation. The residue of My people shall plunder them, and the remnant of My people shall possess them." This they shall have for their pride, because they have reproached and made arrogant threats against the people of the LORD of hosts* (Zephaniah 2:9-10 NKJV).

*But they shall fly down upon the shoulder of the Philistines toward the west; together they shall plunder the people of the East; they shall **lay their hand on Edom and Moab**; and the people of Ammon shall obey them* (Isaiah 11:14 NKJV).

*Against Moab. Thus says the LORD of hosts, the God of Israel: "Woe to Nebo! For it is plundered, **Kirjathaim is shamed and taken**; the high stronghold is shamed and dismayed"* (Jeremiah 48:1 NKJV).

GOD'S NAME, JEHOVAH, WILL BE EXALTED

God's name, Jehovah, will be exalted among the nations: "Thus I will magnify Myself and sanctify Myself, and I will be known in the eyes of many nations. Then they shall know that I am the LORD" (Ezek. 38:23 NKJV).

Several of the prophecies in the Old Testament seem to reveal a consistent progression of activity in the Last Days, for example:

Ezekiel 36:1-15. The restoration of the land of Israel.

Ezekiel 37:1-10. The resurrection of the dry bones of Israel

Ezekiel 37:10. An exceedingly great Israeli Army. (Also Ps. 83; Joel 3:1-3.)

Zechariah 12:1-3. Jerusalem attracts worldwide attention.

Zechariah 12:4-6. A military attack on Israel.

Zechariah 12:5-9. God defends Israel defeating her enemies.

Zechariah 12:10-14. The Messiah reveals Himself to Israel

Zechariah 12:10. The spirit of grace and supplication upon Israel.

Zechariah 13:1-6. A time of revival for Israel. (Also Joel 2:18-27.)

Joel 2:28-32. A world wide spiritual revival/harvest.

Ezekiel 38–39. The war of Gog and Magog.

Daniel 7-12; Revelation 7:14. The Great Tribulation.

Ezekiel 40-48. The Millennial Kingdom on earth.

Revelation 20:7-9. Satan loosed for a little while. (Armageddon?)

Revelation 21–22. The eternal Kingdom of God on earth.

The (soon) coming of Messiah, an event toward which the final stages of this era are rapidly moving, will take place in an environment of great tribulation and ensuing pressures. During this period the gospel of the Kingdom will be preached to all nations on earth and millions of people from every false religion will flood into the Kingdom of God. Worldwide evangelism will flourish with great signs, wonders, and miracles. Believers around the globe need to call upon God for the faith, grace, and strength to endure. He will not only give faith to survive and overcome, He will give faith to triumph and be gloriously victorious. We must urge and encourage every Christian to continue strong in the faith as did the apostles.

> *And when they had preached the gospel to that city and made many disciples, they returned to Lystra, Iconium, and Antioch, strengthening the souls of the disciples, exhorting them to continue in the faith, and saying, "We must through many* **tribulations** *[Gk: thlipsis] enter the kingdom of God"* (Acts 14:21-22 NKJV).

THE EMERGING KINGDOM

No Bible student with an unbiased mind would deny that the Kingdom company in the Last Days will be comprised of Messianic Jews and believing Gentiles. This reality is seen throughout the Book of Revelation, from Revelation 4:4 to 19:4, where reference is made to 24 elders obviously representing Israel and the Church. The same theme is confirmed in Revelation 7 where the 144,000 (12x12) Jews are sealed with the mark of God and stand beside an innumerable company of Gentiles.

THE ONE NEW MAN

Paul defines the Last Days company as the One New Man.

> *For He Himself is our peace, who has made both one, and has broken down the middle wall of separation, having abolished in His flesh the enmity, that is, the law of commandments contained in ordinances, so as to create in Himself **one new man from the two**, thus making peace, and that He might reconcile them both to God in one body through the cross, thereby putting to death the enmity* (Ephesians 2:14-16 NKJV).

The theocratic government of God (see 1 Samuel 8:7), was established originally through Abraham and continued through David and his seed from which Christ came. This righteous line was established by God to create a distinctive people through whom His purpose might be fulfilled—to rule all nations on earth. Throughout the time from Abraham to Christ, it was obviously a Jewish line with the exception of one or two Gentiles who were included through God's grace. Every covenant that God ever made with humankind was originally made with Israel, including the "New" covenant.

> *"Behold, the days are coming, says the LORD, when I will make **a new covenant with the house of Israel and with the house of Judah"** (Jeremiah 31:31 NKJV).

God always intended that this covenant would also include the Gentiles who would be grafted into the Jewish roots and trunk (see Rom. 11:17-20).

THE KINGDOM OF HEAVEN

God's Kingdom will have its origin, principles, and authority in Heaven, but it will be established on earth from the throne of David in Jerusalem. I believe that King David's greater Son, Yeshua the Messiah of Israel, will reign upon that throne. This name, David's greater Son which is frequently used with reference to the Messiah, emphatically confirms that Jesus the Messiah is a legitimate descendant of King David. Both Matthew and Luke painstakingly emphasize the ancestral lines of Jesus giving clear evidence of His kingly origin according to the flesh. Unless this was so, Jesus could never be recognized by Israel as the true Messiah. However, it further affirms that although He is a descendant of David, He is actually greater in every respect than His royal ancestor. This earthly kingdom will be established first through Israel the people who shall be regathered, redeemed, and restored. The regathering will be from the ends of the earth, from every place to which they have been scattered throughout the world. Once back in their land, they will be restored as a sovereign nation, and finally they will be regenerated and become a Messianic nation after the unveiling of Messiah as stated in Zechariah 12:10.

The outpouring of God's Spirit on Israel (see Zech. 12:10) will *precede* the promised outpouring on *all* flesh. It will initiate the Messianic army of Israel and the One New Man.

> *And it shall come to pass afterward That I will* **pour out My Spirit** *on all flesh; Your sons and your daughters shall prophesy, Your old men shall dream dreams, Your young men shall see visions. And also on My menservants and on My maidservants I will pour out My Spirit in those days* (Joel 2:28-29 NKJV).

This outpouring of the Holy Spirit, with grace and supplications upon the inhabitants of Jerusalem (Jews, Christians, and former Muslims), will initiate the greatest harvest that humankind has ever witnessed. All will have a Messianic and Kingdom vision and will powerfully proclaim the true "Gospel of the Kingdom" with all manner of supernatural evidences. In addition to powerful signs, wonders, and miracles, the major evidence will be the unity between the Jews, Christians, and former Muslims involved.

GOD'S BRILLIANT STRATEGY

The greatest political and social problem in our world today is the animosity between the Muslim and non-Muslim worlds. This is particularly true in the Middle East where various Islamic agencies are striving fervently for control of Jerusalem. The city of Jerusalem, where the Jewish Temple Mount has been surmounted by the Dome of the Rock which dominates the skyline of the ancient city, is the prime target of Islam.

How brilliant is God's strategy of pouring out His Spirit on Jews, Muslims, and Christians in the city and establishing a prominent international city where all three families of Abraham will live together in harmony. I believe that the spiritual vibrations from that city will reverberate around the world and will bring hope and salvation that will impact all the nations on earth. I also believe that millions of Muslims worldwide will come to faith in Yeshua the Jewish Messiah who is also the commander of the armies of the LORD.

It is my opinion that all will be submitted to the Messiah who will be Lord and King. A spiritual army which includes Jews, Christians, and former Muslims will exercise an exceedingly powerful ministry throughout the world. The inherent deeper Jewish understanding of Hebraic inferences and implications in the Gospel message, together with the intense commitment to the cause which is exemplified by previously Muslim believers will give tremendous strength and authority to the message of the Kingdom. Christian believers will shake off the shackles and limitations of institutional religion and commit themselves wholly in complete abandonment to the authentic liberation and authority of the vibrant message that Jesus originally commissioned us to proclaim.

The Body of Christ universal will reap a tremendous harvest into the Kingdom of God. The King will truly reign on the earth through the citizens of His Kingdom. The Body will not be weak and anemic as the institutional church has been. It will be mighty, strong, and influential in the awesome power of God's Spirit. This latter day outpouring of the Holy Spirit will not only be "life from the dead" for Israel (see Rom. 11:15), it will also be like a new resurrection for the Church. God will breathe new life into the Church again, and this will be like a second Pentecost.

Those believers who respond to the call of God in this prophetic time zone will arise from the grave of dead tradition in a newness of life. Church traditions, rites, rules, and sacred buildings will be vacated and believers will once again go into the highways and byways and compel men and women into God's Kingdom family. The Body of Christ will no longer be as a dead corpse. It will throb again with new life and zest.

Chapter Eleven

ISRAEL'S GLORIOUS RESTORATION

And I will pour on the house of David and on the inhabitants of Jerusalem the Spirit of grace and supplication; then they will look on Me whom they pierced. Yes, they will mourn for Him as one mourns for his only son, and grieve for Him as one grieves for a firstborn (Zechariah 12:10 NKJV).

God has made many amazing and glorious prophetic promises to Israel. As you know by now, I believe that Zechariah 12:10 predicts a more potently powerful event than anyone has yet envisaged. It not only forecasts an astounding military victory for Israel which against all odds delivers them from national annihilation, *it also predicts the subsequent recognition of their Messiah as the source of the victory and the amazing transformation of Israel as a direct result of that recognition.*

One of the unique things about Zechariah 12:10 is the manifestation of what Christians have long called the Trinity—Jehovah (1) pours forth His Spirit (2) and reveals the Messiah (3). The issue concerning the Trinity has always been a major controversy between Muslims, Jews, and Gentiles. In this verse, the three aspects of the one God are plainly seen.

As mentioned previously, one of the amazing New Testament predictions concerning Israel is that in the Last Days she will ultimately be regrafted back into the olive tree from which she was broken off (see Rom. 11:17). This is the very same tree into which the Gentile believers have already been grafted. This regrafting of Israel will mean a solid uniting together of Jew and Gentile believers in Yeshua the Jewish Messiah.

> *And if the Jews turn from their unbelief, God will graft them back into the tree again. He has the power to do it* (Romans 11:23). (See also Romans 11:17,19, and 24.)

When Paul says *"if the Jews turn from their unbelief,"* he is obviously referring to their unbelief concerning Jesus being the Jewish Messiah, which is an underlying theme of the Book of Romans. Following the sensational, supernatural victory that Messiah will achieve for Israel (see Zech. 12:9-10), and the subsequent unveiling of His identity, there will surely be no more unbelief concerning Him. They will not see Him in the way in which the Gentiles have seen Him thus far, and the Gentile comprehension of Messiah will also change dramatically as they witness the regrafting of Israel.

I believe that Israel will be regrafted onto their own olive tree at that time. This event also appears to provide the ideal situation in which the spiritual restoration of Israel could happen. The Messiah they have long failed to recognize will suddenly appear as the commander-in-chief of their armed forces and procure for them an amazing supernatural victory averting the possibility of national annihilation. God will also pour upon them His Spirit of grace, intercessions, and revelation, making them extremely compliant to the revelation of His unique Jewish identity.

There are many other Scriptures that clearly indicate a powerful spiritual restoration of Israel in the context of the End Times. One of these occurs in the writings of Paul to the Gentile church in Rome. He likens Israel's restoration to an explosive resurrection from the dead. A whole nation will at one time be raised from the grave of a superseded religious system to be eternally energized by the Spirit of the living God.

> *Now if their fall is riches for the world, and their failure riches for the Gentiles,* **how much more** *[will their] **their fullness** [be]! For I speak to you Gentiles; inasmuch as I am an apostle to the Gentiles, I magnify my ministry, if by any means I may provoke to jealousy those who are my flesh and save some of them. For if their*

being cast away is the reconciling of the world, **what will their acceptance be but life from the dead?** (Romans 11:12-15 NKJV)

Paul refers to the "fullness" of Israel. The word translated fullness
is *pleroma* which Paul uses in several other places. He also intimates
that one of the God-given tasks of the Gentiles is to provoke the
Jews to jealousy to the extent that they will desire a unity with the
Gentiles in the Messiah. This is a task that many Gentiles have so far
failed to address or achieve.

CHRIST ARRIVED IN THE "FULLNESS OF TIME"

But when the fullness [pleroma] *of the time had come, God sent
forth His Son, born of a woman, born under the law, to redeem
those who were under the law, that we might receive the adop-
tion as sons* (Galatians 4:4-5 NKJV).

In Galatians 4:4, the fullness or *pleroma* was obviously a predeter-
mined and absolutely critical moment in time—the most decisive
and appropriate time for the Messiah to be born. Jesus came to the
world when it was the most timely for Him to come. The fullness of
time refers to the most suitable and appropriate time. Everything
was made ready for His appearance. And now at the closure of this
age, again at the most supremely appropriate moment, He will appear once again to save Israel from the threat of total destruction
and to impart new resurrection life to the nation.

Paul further speaks of the fullness of time when God will gather
together all things in Heaven and earth under the headship of Christ.

That in the **dispensation of the fullness of the times** *He might
gather together in one all things in Christ, both which are in heaven
and which are on earth—in Him* (Ephesians 1:10 NKJV).

Once again, at the most timely moment in history, God is going to
gather all things together in Christ the Messiah. The world will eventually bear witness to just how appropriate that moment will be when
the Messiah unveils Himself again to Israel. This time Israel will recognize Him by divine revelation and they will proudly bear His name.

Ephesians 1:10 states that in the *pleroma* of times God will *gather together in one all things in Christ*. This statement obviously includes Jew and Gentile being brought into unity in Christ as in Ephesians 2:15: "having abolished in His flesh the enmity, that is, the law of commandments contained in ordinances, **so as to create in Himself one new man from the two, thus making peace**" (NKJV).

> *Till we all* [Jew and Gentile] *come to the unity of the faith and of the knowledge of the Son of God, to a perfect man, to the measure of the stature of the* **fullness** [pleroma] *of Christ* (Ephesians 4:13 NKJV).

Ephesians 4:13 refers to a (prophetic) time when the Body of Christ comes together in the unity of the faith which equates to *the measure of the stature of the fullness of Christ*. This will be the prophetic moment when Jew and Gentile combine to manifest the One New Man. In the consistent context of Ephesians, Paul emphasizes that through the death of Christ, God has broken down forever the wall that separated Jew from Gentile and has caused them to be one. Paul, the apostle to the Gentiles, does not want any of the Gentiles to be ignorant of this mystery—that Jew and Gentile have been reconciled to each other through the death of Christ.

> *By His death He ended the whole system of Jewish law that excluded the Gentiles. His purpose was to make peace between Jews and Gentiles by creating in Himself one new person from the two groups. Together as one body, Christ reconciled both groups to God by means of his death, and our hostility toward each other was put to death. He has brought this Good News of peace to you Gentiles who were far away from Him, and to us Jews who were near. Now all of us, both Jews and Gentiles, may come to the Father through the same Holy Spirit because of what Christ has done for us* (Ephesians 2:15-18).

Paul also wants the Gentiles to understand another mystery: the spiritual blindness of Israel is both partial and temporary. Their blindness and hardness of heart will be instantly healed when the Deliverer turns Israel from all ungodliness and keeps His covenant promise to take away all their sins.

*For I would not, brethren, that ye should be ignorant of this mystery, lest ye should be wise in your own conceits; that blindness in part is happened to Israel, until the **fullness** [pleroma] **of the Gentiles be come in**. And so all Israel shall be saved: as it is written, there shall come out of Sion the Deliverer, and shall turn away ungodliness from Jacob: for this is my covenant unto them, when I shall take away their sins* (Romans 11:25-27 KJV).

It seems quite evident in all these references that fullness or pleroma does not refer to a mathematical sum total but rather to a predicted moment in time. So in Romans 11, Paul is referring to a prophetic *pleroma* moment for both Israel and the Gentiles. Might this not be the same prophetic moment? The ultimate fullness of both the Jewish and Gentile believers in Messiah will occur through their unity with each other. One will not exist without the other. This unity and togetherness of Jew and Gentile is the basic theme of this whole chapter. The conclusion of the chapter is that all Israel shall be saved (see Rom. 11:26).

There are numerous other biblical passages concerning Israel's future that do not seem to fit into either the present era, nor into the Millennium. There are many passages of prophetic Scripture that foretell amazing things that God will accomplish for Israel to redeem the honor of His name. None of these Scriptures have any specific intimation that they will not happen until the Millennium.

Do these passages suggest that there may be a period of time in God's prophetic purpose that is largely unaccounted for in the popular End Times scenarios? Is it an era that is better than the present one, but not as good as the ultimate one? Is it a hiatus in time when Israel will experience and manifest the glorious blessings that God has reserved for His ancient covenant people? And could that time be the same period that Zechariah 12:10 predicts will immediately follow the amazing victory that the Messiah achieves for Israel?

Too many Christian theologians and commentators have been too hasty to ascribe all positive promises of blessing and glory upon Israel to the Millennial period. Many such Scriptures do not fit well into the Millennial period. Several of them mention "ruling the nations with a rod of iron" etc. and God destroying nations, which may not suggest that they happen in the atmosphere of peace achieved by the Millennial reign of Christ. These passages probably indicate some future period between the present time and the ultimate eternal purpose, when Israel and the Church will be blessed in a far greater measure than is presently the case, but is yet still far short of what God has promised will ultimately happen.

All too frequently Israel's future has been painted in dark sombre colors of tragedy and grief. Too many commentators have assumed that God's intended glorious future for Israel has been completely cancelled out because the whole nation did not embrace Jesus as the Jewish Messiah. The reality, however, is very different. The Bible portrays a glorious future of hope for Israel that will definitely occur, not because Israel is somehow deserving of it, but because God intends to demonstrate the limitless extent of His grace, mercy, and faithfulness through His treatment of Israel.

> *"There is hope for your future,"* says the LORD. *"Your children will come again to their own land. I have heard Israel saying, 'You disciplined me severely, but I deserved it. I was like a calf that needed to be trained for the yoke and plow. Turn me again to you and restore me, for you alone are the LORD my God. I turned away from God, but then I was sorry. I kicked myself for my stupidity! I was thoroughly ashamed of all I did in my younger days.' Is not Israel still My son, My darling child?"* asks the LORD. *"I had to punish him, but I still love him. I long for him and surely will have mercy on him"*(Jeremiah 31:17-20 GNT).

The hope that God predicts for Israel is expressed in the Hebrew word *tikvah* which basically means, the hopeful expectation of the thing that I long for. Throughout the long years of Israel's scattering in the Diaspora, God's chosen people have been severely disciplined. However, those years of discipline are almost over now, and God is about to restore Israel to the experience of His favor. The long years of Israel's difficult history have all constituted a training program for Israel. I believe that God has been preparing them for the years when they, with their King David and the Messiah, will rule and reign from Jerusalem.

I will watch over and care for them, and I will bring them back here again. I will build them up and not tear them down. I will plant them and not uproot them. I will give them hearts that recognize me as the LORD. They will be My people, and I will be their God, for they will return to Me wholeheartedly (Jeremiah 24:6-7).

Hope in the English dictionary signifies expectation, optimism, something to wish for. Therefore, if we hope for something, we wish that it would happen. But hope, in its biblical sense, means assurance, confidence, and certainty. However, it will only be this if we have active faith and this depends on who made the promise. We can only hope (wish) that man will keep his promise; but when the promise is made by God, we can fully trust with utmost confidence that the hope will be fulfilled.

The hope (see Jer. 31:17) that has sustained Israel throughout her tempestuous history is expressed in the current national anthem of Israel aptly named Ha Tikvah—The Hope.

> *As long as deep in the heart,*
> *The soul of a Jew yearns,*
> *And forward to the East*
> *To Zion, an eye looks*
> *Our hope will not be lost,*
> *The hope of two thousand years,*
> *To be a free nation in our land,*
> *The land of Zion and Jerusalem.*

THE FULFILLMENT OF THE YEARNING

Yes, I will rejoice over them to do them good, and I will assuredly plant them in this land, with all My heart and with all My soul. "For thus says the LORD: 'Just as I have brought all this great calamity on this people, so I will bring on them all the good that I have promised them'" (Jeremiah 32:41-42 NKJV).

Jehovah's expectation for Israel's future is obviously very positive and good. He predicts that He will rejoice to do Israel good as He faithfully and wholeheartedly replants them in their land. God has certainly not brought the Jewish people back to their land to see them decimated or destroyed. He has brought them back with one purpose in mind, to do them good and to vindicate the honor of His name. As certain as curses and calamities have historically overtaken Israel, so it is also absolutely certain that the blessings of God will finally come upon them.

My desire and purpose is to bring attention to some of the prophetic passages that predict glorious things predicted upon Israel. Please consider the very real possibility that just as many of God's prophecies have been fulfilled since 1948, many more breathtaking prophecies will be fulfilled in the very near future after the Messiah reveals Himself afresh to Israel as stated in Zechariah 12:10.

ISRAEL'S RESTORATION

Israel's restoration is predicted in Deuteronomy 30:

Suppose all these things happen to you—the blessings and the curses I have listed—and you meditate on them as you are living among the nations to which the LORD your God has exiled you. If at that time you return to the LORD your God, and you and your children begin wholeheartedly to obey all the commands I have given you today, then the LORD your God will restore your fortunes. He will have mercy on you and gather you back from all the nations where He has scattered you. Though you are at the ends of the earth, the LORD your God will go and find you and bring you back again. He will return you to the land that belonged to your ancestors, and you will possess that land again. He will make you even more prosperous and numerous than your ancestors! "The LORD your God will cleanse your heart and the hearts of all your descendants so that you will love Him with all your heart and soul, and so you may live! The LORD your God will inflict all these curses on your enemies and persecutors. Then you will again obey the LORD and keep all the commands I am giving you today. The LORD your God will make you successful in everything you do. He will give you many children and numerous livestock, and your fields will produce abundant harvests, for the LORD will delight in being good to you as He was to your

ancestors. The LORD your God will delight in you if you obey
His voice and keep the commands and laws written in this Book
of the Law, and if you turn to the LORD your God with all your
heart and soul (Deuteronomy 3:1-10).

This Scripture passage predicts the restoration of Israel to Jehovah. It will be a brand-new era in the life of the nation who will obey Him with all their heart, mind, and soul. The promises contained in it were given to Israel immediately prior to their entry into their Promised Land. I believe they are also very relevant to Israel now as God prepares to bring Israel into her predicted restoration and new beginning.

Some results of Israel's restoration predicted in Deuteronomy 30 include:

- Regathering from the Diaspora. (Deut. 30:3-5)
- Judgment upon her enemies. (Deut. 30:7)
- Wholehearted love for God. (Deut. 30:6)
- Wholehearted obedience to God. (Deut. 30:2)
- Restoration to their ancient homeland with restored fortunes. (Deut. 30:3-5)
- Success and prosperity. (Deut. 30:9)
- Curses on those who have cursed Israel. (Deut. 30:7)

Jeremiah confirms this restoration in glowing terminology. He portrays for Israel redemption, joyful singing and dancing, prosperity, radiance, rejoicing, and a future that will be "like a well watered garden." This might suggest a restoration of an Edenic kind of shalom.

Jeremiah and Zechariah make several wonderful predictions concerning Israel's future:

In that day Jerusalem will be known as The Throne of the
LORD. All nations will come there to honor the LORD. They
will no longer stubbornly follow their own evil desires. In those
days the people of Judah and Israel will return together from
exile in the north. They will return to the land I gave their ances-
tors as an inheritance forever (Jeremiah 3:17-18).

"Yes, we will come," the people reply, "for you are the LORD our God. Our worship of idols and our religious orgies on the hills and mountains are completely false. Only in the LORD our God will Israel ever find salvation" (Jeremiah 3:22-23).

*"Listen to this message from the LORD, you nations of the world; proclaim it in distant coastlands: The LORD, who scattered His people, will gather them together and watch over them as a shepherd does his flock. For the LORD has redeemed Israel from those too strong for them. They will come home and sing songs of joy on the heights of Jerusalem. They will be radiant because of the many gifts the LORD has given them—the good crops of wheat, wine, and oil, and the healthy flocks and herds. **Their life will be like a watered garden, and all their sorrows will be gone.** The young women will dance for joy, and the men—old and young—will join in the celebration. I will turn their mourning into joy. I will comfort them and exchange their sorrow for rejoicing. I will supply the priests with an abundance of offerings. I will satisfy My people with My bounty. I, the LORD, have spoken!"* (Jeremiah 31:10-14)

Then another message came to me from the LORD Almighty: "This is what the LORD Almighty says: My love for Mount Zion is passionate and strong; I am consumed with passion for Jerusalem! And now the LORD says: I am returning to Mount Zion, and I will live in Jerusalem. Then Jerusalem will be called the Faithful City; the mountain of the LORD Almighty will be called the Holy Mountain. This is what the LORD Almighty says: Once again old men and women will walk Jerusalem's streets with a cane and sit together in the city squares. And the streets of the city will be filled with boys and girls at play" (Zechariah 8:1-5).

God is filled with passionate, strong love for Mount Zion in Jerusalem where He will make His abode. It is the LORD Almighty— El Shaddai who makes this positive declaration.

"So do not be afraid, Jacob, my servant; do not be dismayed, Israel, says the LORD. For I will bring you home again from distant

lands, and your children will return from their exile. Israel will return and will have peace and quiet in their own land, and no one will make them afraid. For I am with you and will save you," says the LORD. "I will completely destroy the nations where I have scattered you, but I will not destroy you. But I must discipline you; I cannot let you go unpunished" (Jeremiah 30:10-11).

In verse 11, the Hebrew word for save is Yasha (H3467) meaning to open wide to free and succour. It is a very potent word having the connotations of rescue, deliver, avenge, defend, help, preserve, make safe. i.e To bring (having) salvation, save (-iour), get victory.[1] All of these implications are exceedingly positive for Israel's future well-being.

Look! The LORD is coming from far away, burning with anger, surrounded by a thick, rising smoke. His lips are filled with fury; His words consume like fire. His anger pours out like a flood on His enemies, sweeping them all away. He will sift out the proud nations. He will bridle them and lead them off to their destruction. But the people of God will sing a song of joy, like the songs at the holy festivals. You will be filled with joy, as when a flutist leads a group of pilgrims to Jerusalem—the mountain of the LORD—to the Rock of Israel (Isaiah 30:27-30).

In Isaiah 30:27-28, Jehovah will appear seeking vengeance for Israel with burning anger and words that consume like a blazing fire. His anger is poured forth on His enemies as He leads them to destruction. During the same time period, the people of God (Israel) will sing a song of joy as at the (ancient) holy festivals when a flutist will lead groups of pilgrims to Jerusalem, to the mountain of the LORD—to "the Rock of Israel."

The apostle Paul refers to the rock from which the Israelites drank in the wilderness and he tells us that amazingly that rock is Christ. Does Isaiah predict that once again Israel will come with music and singing to the mountain of the LORD, even the Rock of Israel?

And all of them ate the same miraculous food, and all of them drank the same miraculous water. For they all drank from the miraculous rock that traveled with them, and that rock was Christ (1 Corinthians 10:3-4).

And you will live in Israel, the land I gave your ancestors long ago. You will be My people, and I will be your God. I will cleanse you of your filthy behavior. I will give you good crops, and I will abolish famine in the land. I will give you great harvests from your fruit trees and fields, and never again will the surrounding nations be able to scoff at your land for its famines. Then you will remember your past sins and hate yourselves for all the evil things you did. But remember, says the Sovereign LORD, I am not doing this because you deserve it. O My people of Israel, you should be utterly ashamed of all you have done! This is what the Sovereign LORD says: When I cleanse you from your sins, I will bring people to live in your cities, and the ruins will be rebuilt. The fields that used to lie empty and desolate—a shock to all who passed by—will again be farmed. And when I bring you back, people will say, "This godforsaken land is now like Eden's garden! The ruined cities now have strong walls, and they are filled with people!" Then the nations all around—all those still left—will know that I, the LORD, rebuilt the ruins and planted lush crops in the wilderness. For I, the LORD, have promised this, and I will do it. This is what the Sovereign LORD says: I am ready to hear Israel's prayers for these blessings, and I am ready to grant them their requests. I will multiply them like the sacred flocks that fill Jerusalem's streets at the time of her festivals. The ruined cities will be crowded with people once more, and everyone will know that I am the LORD (Ezekiel 36:28-38).

In that day Judah will be saved, and Jerusalem will live in safety. And their motto will be "The LORD [Jehovah] is our righteousness!" For this is what the LORD says: David will forever have a descendant sitting on the throne of Israel. And there will always be Levitical priests to offer burnt offerings and grain offerings and sacrifices to Me" (Jeremiah 33:16-18).

The following passage of Scripture tells of two kings who will reign from the throne of David. I believe the first portion (verses 21-25) refers to David the King who will reign over Israel. The second sequence (verses 26-28) refers to the Messiah King, who will rule over all the nations on earth.

KING DAVID'S REIGN OVER ISRAEL

*And give them this message from the Sovereign LORD: I will gather the people of Israel from among the nations. I will bring them home to their own land from the places where they have been scattered. I will unify them into one nation in the land. One king will rule them all; no longer will they be divided into two nations. They will stop polluting themselves with their detestable idols and other sins, for I will save them from their sinful back-sliding. I will cleanse them. Then they will truly be My people, and I will be their God. "My servant David will be their king, and they will have only one shepherd. They will obey My regulations and keep My laws. They will live in the land of Israel where their ancestors lived, the land I gave My servant Jacob. They and their children and their grandchildren after them will live there forever, generation after generation. **And My servant David will be their prince forever**"* (Ezekiel 37:21-25).

In that day I will restore the fallen kingdom of David. It is now like a house in ruins, but I will rebuild its walls and restore its former glory. And Israel will possess what is left of Edom and all the nations I have called to be Mine. I, the LORD, have spoken, and I will do these things (Amos 9:11-12).

Then God will establish one of David's descendants as king. He will rule with mercy and truth. He will always do what is just and be eager to do what is right (Isaiah 16:5).

In various prophetic scriptures David is called a king (see Ezek. 37:24), but he is also called a prince, (see Ezek. 37:25). He will be the king over Israel and a prince over the nations under the King Messiah. I believe that initially King David will rule over the twelve tribes of Israel from his throne in Jerusalem. Later, following His Second advent, the Messiah will reign over all the nations that remain on earth. David will be His prince.

THE MESSIAH'S REIGN OVER ALL NATIONS

A king like My servant David will be their king. They will all be united under one ruler and will obey My laws faithfully. They will live on the land I gave to My servant Jacob, the land where their ancestors lived. They will live there forever, and so will their children and all their descendants. A king like My servant David will rule them forever. I will make a covenant with them that guarantees their security forever. I will establish them and increase their population, and will see to it that My Temple stands forever in their land. I will live there with them; I will be their God, and they will be My people. When I place My Temple there to be among them forever, then the nations will know that I, the LORD, have chosen Israel to be My own people (Ezekiel 36:24-28 GNT).

A child is born to us! A son is given to us! And He will be our ruler. He will be called, "Wonderful Counselor," "Mighty God," "Eternal Father," "Prince of Peace." His royal power will continue to grow; His kingdom will always be at peace. He will rule as King David's successor, basing His power on right and justice, from now until the end of time. The LORD Almighty is determined to do all this (Isaiah 9:6-7 GNT).

"When that time comes, Jerusalem will be called 'The Throne of the LORD,' and all nations will gather there to worship Me. They will no longer do what their stubborn and evil hearts tell them. Israel will join with Judah, and together they will come from exile in the country in the north and will return to the land that I gave your ancestors as a permanent possession." The LORD says, "Israel, I wanted to accept you as My child and give you a delightful land, the most beautiful land in all the world. I wanted you to call Me Father and never again turn away from Me" (Jeremiah 3:17-19 GNT). (See also Jeremiah 3:17-18, 23:5-6; Ezekiel 37:26-28.)

God promises to Israel:

- An eternal covenant of peace.
- The original Promised Land of expanded Israel.
- A multiplication of the population.
- A temple in their midst.
- God will dwell among them.
- He will be their God and they shall be His people.

- All the nations will recognize that Israel is God's holy nation.

"I will bring My exiled people of Israel back from distant lands, and they will rebuild their ruined cities and live in them again. They will plant vineyards and gardens; they will eat their crops and drink their wine. I will firmly plant them there in the land I have given them," says the LORD your God. "Then they will never be uprooted again" (Amos 9:14-15).

- Exiles will return to Israel from distant lands.
- They will rebuild (ancient) ruined cities.
- They will plant, harvest, and enjoy vineyards and gardens.
- They will never be uprooted from Israel again.

I will sow them among the peoples, and they shall remember Me in far countries; they shall live, together with their children, and they shall return. I will also bring them back from the land of Egypt, and gather them from Assyria. I will bring them into the land of Gilead and Lebanon, until no more room is found for them (Zechariah 10:9-10 NKJV).

GOD'S CONCERN FOR HIS HOLY NAME

Everything that God accomplishes for Israel will rebound to the honor of His sacred name.

Then I was concerned for My holy name, which had been dishonored by My people throughout the world. "Therefore, give the people of Israel this message from the Sovereign LORD: I am bringing you back again but not because you deserve it. I am doing it to protect my holy name, which you dishonored while you were scattered among the nations. I will show how holy My great name is—the name you dishonored among the nations. And when I reveal my holiness through you before their very eyes, says the Sovereign LORD, then the nations will know that I am the LORD. For I will gather you up from all the nations and bring you home again to your land (Ezekiel 36:21-24). (See also Ezekiel 20:9, Ezekiel 36:32, Isaiah 43:25, Ezekiel 20:14.)

ISRAEL—A SWEET AROMA TO GOD

As the Levitical priesthood offered, among their many sacrifices, a sweet incense to the LORD, so Israel, as a newly sanctified nation, will become a sweet aroma in the nostrils of the LORD.

> *"I will accept you as a sweet aroma when I bring you out from the peoples and gather you out of the countries where you have been scattered; and I will be hallowed in you before the Gentiles. Then you shall know that I am the LORD, when I bring you into the land of Israel, into the country for which I raised My hand in an oath to give to your fathers. And there you shall remember your ways and all your doings with which you were defiled; and you shall loathe yourselves in your own sight because of all the evils that you have committed. Then you shall know that I am the LORD, when I have dealt with you for My name's sake, not according to your wicked ways nor according to your corrupt doings, O house of Israel," says the Lord GOD* (Ezekiel 20:41-44 NKJV).

MORE PROSPEROUS THAN THEIR ANCESTORS

> *"Suppose all these things happen to you—the blessings and the curses I have listed—and you meditate on them as you are living among the nations to which the LORD your God has exiled you. If at that time you return to the LORD your God, and you and your children begin wholeheartedly to obey all the commands I have given you today, then the LORD your God will restore your fortunes. He will have mercy on you and gather you back from all the nations where He has scattered you. Though you are at the ends of the earth, the LORD your God will go and find you and bring you back again. He will return you to the land that belonged to your ancestors, and you will possess that land again. He will make you even more prosperous and numerous than your ancestors!"* (Deuteronomy 30:1-5)

Under the reign of King Solomon, the nation enjoyed enormous wealth and prosperity; but when King David is restored to his throne, Israel will inherit greater wealth and prosperity than ever before.

King Solomon's reign was not only a time of great material prosperity and amazing wealth, it was also a renaissance of intellectual activity particularly in the arts and sciences. The fame of Solomon's brilliant wisdom spread far and wide throughout the world. Among his great admirers was the queen of Sheba who visited Solomon in Jerusalem to imbibe his wisdom and knowledge. She was filled with amazement by all she saw and heard: "there was no more spirit in her." After an exchange of presents, she returned to her native land.

When the queen of Sheba realized how wise Solomon was, and when she saw the palace he had built, she was breathless. She was also amazed at the food on his tables, the organization of his officials and their splendid clothing, the cup-bearers and their robes, and the burnt offerings Solomon made at the Temple of the LORD. She exclaimed to the king, "Everything I heard in my country about your achievements and wisdom is true! I didn't believe it until I arrived here and saw it with my own eyes. Truly I had not heard the half of it! Your wisdom and prosperity are far greater than what I was told. How happy these people must be! What a privilege for your officials to stand here day after day, listening to your wisdom! The LORD your God is great indeed! He delights in you and has placed you on the throne of Israel. Because the LORD loves Israel with an eternal love, He has made you king so you can rule with justice and righteousness" (1 Kings 10:4-9).

KINGS AND RULERS WILL SERVE ISRAEL

*This is what the Sovereign LORD says: "See, I will give a signal to the godless nations. They will carry your little sons back to you in their arms; they will bring your daughters on their shoulders. **Kings and queens will serve you**. They will care for all your needs. They will bow to the earth before you and lick the dust from your feet. Then you will know that I am the LORD. Those who wait for Me will never be put to shame"* (Isaiah 49:22-23). (See also Isaiah 60:10-13, Isaiah 60:14-18.)

MIRACLES MIGHTIER THAN THE EXODUS

O LORD, come and rule Your people; lead your flock in green pastures. Help them to live in peace and prosperity. Let them enjoy the fertile pastures of Bashan and Gilead as they did long ago. "Yes," says the LORD, "I will do mighty miracles for you, like those I did when I rescued you from slavery in Egypt." All the nations of the world will stand amazed at what the LORD will do for you. They will be embarrassed that their power is so insignificant. They will stand in silent awe, deaf to everything around them. They will come to realize what lowly creatures they really are. Like snakes crawling from their holes, they will come out to meet the LORD our God. They will fear Him greatly, trembling in terror at His presence (Micah 7:14-17).

GOD'S GRACE, MERCY, AND COMPASSION ON ISRAEL

The response of Israel toward God will be encouraged and occasioned by the Spirit (Ruach) of grace that He pours upon them.

But the LORD will have mercy on the descendants of Jacob. Israel will be His special people once again. He will bring them back to settle once again in their own land. And people from many different nations will come and join them there and become a part of the people of Israel. The nations of the world will help the LORD's people to return, and those who come to live in their land will serve them. Those who captured Israel will be captured, and Israel will rule over its enemies (Isaiah 14:1-2).

UPROOTING EVIL NATIONS

Now this is what the LORD says: "I will uproot from their land all the evil nations reaching out for the possession I gave My people Israel. And I will uproot Judah from among them. But afterward I will return and have compassion on all of them. I will bring them home to their own lands again, each nation to its own inheritance. And if these nations quickly learn the ways of my people, and if they learn to swear by My name, saying, 'As surely as the LORD lives' (just as they taught my people to swear by the name of Baal), then they will be given a place among my people. But any nation who refuses to obey Me will be uprooted and destroyed. I, the LORD, have spoken!" (Jeremiah 12:14-17)

True, many nations have gathered together against you, calling for your blood, eager to gloat over your destruction. But they do not know the LORD's thoughts or understand his plan. These nations don't know that He is gathering them together to be beaten and trampled like bundles of grain on a threshing floor (Micah 4:11-12).

THE GREAT SHEPHERD OF ISRAEL

God will gather His sheep together in their ancient homeland and demonstrate His great Shepherd heart for all the world to see.

Listen to this message from the LORD, you nations of the world; proclaim it in distant coastlands: The LORD, who scattered His people, will gather them together and watch over them as a shepherd does his flock. For the LORD has redeemed Israel from those too strong for them (Jeremiah 31:10-11). (See also Ezekiel 34:11-16; 34:23-24.)

A CITY OF REFUGE

As the cities of refuge were built to provide shelter and safety for those guilty of manslaughter, so Jerusalem will provide a refuge for all who seek solace and safety.

But Jerusalem will become a refuge for those who escape; it will be a holy place. And the people of Israel will come back to reclaim their inheritance. At that time Israel will be a raging fire, and Edom, a field of dry stubble. The fire will roar across the field, devouring everything and leaving no survivors in Edom. I, the LORD, have spoken! Then my people living in the Negev will occupy the mountains of Edom. Those living in the foothills of Judah will possess the Philistine plains and take over the fields of Ephraim and Samaria. And the people of Benjamin will occupy the land of Gilead. The exiles of Israel will return to their land

and occupy the Phoenician coast as far north as Zarephath. The captives from Jerusalem exiled in the north will return to their homeland and resettle the villages of the Negev. Deliverers will go up to Mount Zion in Jerusalem to rule over the mountains of Edom. And the LORD himself will be king! (Obadiah 17-21)

THE RADIANT CITY
(CONTEMPORARY ENGLISH VERSION)

Jerusalem, stand up! Shine! Your new day is dawning. The glory of the LORD shines brightly on you. The earth and its people are covered with darkness, but the glory of the LORD is shining upon you (Isaiah 60:1-2 CEV).

All nations will come to your light. Mighty kings will come to see your radiance. "Look and see, for everyone is coming home! Your sons are coming from distant lands; your little daughters will be carried home. Your eyes will shine, and your hearts will thrill with joy, for merchants from around the world will come to you. They will bring you the wealth of many lands. Vast caravans of camels will converge on you, the camels of Midian and Ephah. From Sheba they will bring gold and incense for the worship of the LORD. The flocks of Kedar will be given to you, and the rams of Nebaioth will be brought for my altars. In that day I will make my Temple glorious. And what do I see flying like clouds to Israel, like doves to their nests? They are the ships of Tarshish, reserved to bring the people of Israel home. They will bring their wealth with them, and it will bring great honor to the LORD your God, the Holy One of Israel, for He will fill you with splendor" (Isaiah 60:3-9). (See also Isaiah 60:12; 60:16-17, Isaiah 54:1-3.)

GODLY LEADERSHIP RESTORED

Although the modern State of Israel has been blessed with some of the most remarkable leaders of the current era, it has also had its share of corruption and deceit among its leadership. In this new era into which God is going to bring the nation, they will have good and godly leaders again.

Then I will give you good judges again and wise counselors like you used to have. Then Jerusalem will again be called the Home of Justice and the Faithful City (Isaiah 1:26).

"They will have their own ruler again, and he will not be a foreigner. I will invite him to approach Me," says the LORD, "for who would dare to come unless invited? You will be My people, and I will be your God" (Jeremiah 30:21-22). (See also Obadiah 21, Jeremiah 23:2-4, Jeremiah 3:15-18.)

PEACE AND SAFETY REIGNS

Everyone will live in peace and prosperity, enjoying their own grapevines and fig trees, for there will be nothing to fear. The Lord of Heaven's Armies has made this promise! Though the nations around us follow their idols, we will follow the Lord our God forever and ever. "In that coming day," says the Lord, "I will gather together those who are lame, those who have been exiles, and those whom I have filled with grief. Those who are weak will survive as a remnant; those who were exiles will become a strong nation. Then I, the Lord, will rule from Jerusalem as their king forever." As for you, Jerusalem, the citadel of God's people, your royal might and power will come back to you again. The kingship will be restored to My precious Jerusalem (Micah 4:4-8). (See also Isaiah 51:3, Isaiah 55:10-13, Joel 3:18-19, Isaiah 4:2, Isaiah 51:11, Isaiah 29:17, Isaiah 30:23-26, Hosea 2:21-23, Joel 2:27, Joel 3:18, Amos 9:13-15.)

BEAUTY FOR ASHES, JOY FOR MOURNING

To all who mourn in Israel, He will give beauty for ashes, joy instead of mourning, praise instead of despair. For the LORD has planted them like strong and graceful oaks for His own glory (Isaiah 61:3).

But now the LORD says, "Do not weep any longer, for I will reward you. Your children will come back to you from the distant land of the enemy. There is hope for your future," says the LORD. "Your children will come again to their own land. I have

*heard Israel saying, 'You disciplined me severely, but I deserved
it. I was like a calf that needed to be trained for the yoke and
plow. Turn me again to You and restore me, for You alone are the
LORD my God. I turned away from God, but then I was sorry.
I kicked myself for my stupidity! I was thoroughly ashamed of
all I did in my younger days.' "Is not Israel still my son, my dar-
ling child?" asks the LORD. "I had to punish him, but I still love
him. I long for him and surely will have mercy on him"* (Jeremiah 31:16-20).

RIGHTEOUS AND JOYFUL CITIZENS

*All your people will be righteous. They will possess their land for-
ever, for I will plant them there with My own hands in order to
bring Myself glory. The smallest family will multiply into a large
clan. The tiniest group will become a mighty nation. I, the LORD,
will bring it all to pass at the right time* (Isaiah 60:21-22). (See
also Jeremiah 31:13-14, Isaiah 33:24, Jeremiah 30:21-24.)

INCREASED POPULATION

*I will make your population grow. You will live in the cities and
rebuild everything that was left in ruins. I will make people and
cattle increase in number. There will be more of you than ever
before, and you will have many children. I will let you live there
as you used to live, and I will make you more prosperous than
ever. Then you will know that I am the LORD. I will bring you,
My people Israel, back to live again in the land. It will be your
own land, and it will never again let your children starve*
(Ezekiel 36:10-12).

*The land will no longer have to listen to the nations making fun
of it or see the peoples sneer at it. The land will no longer rob the
nation of its children. I, the Sovereign LORD, have spoken*
(Ezekiel 36:15 GNT).

One of the saddest features of life in contemporary Israel is the
high rate of abortions, possibly as a result of the tension of living
under so much pressure and uncertainty. How wonderful that God

promises to rectify this when He causes His people to live in peace, safe from the attacks of her numerous enemies.

> *When I demonstrate to the nations the holiness of My great name—the name you disgraced among them—then they will know that I am the LORD. I, the Sovereign LORD, have spoken. I will use you to show the nations that I am holy. I will take you from every nation and country and bring you back to your own land. I will sprinkle clean water on you and make you clean from all your idols and everything else that has defiled you. I will give you a new heart and a new mind. I will take away your stubborn heart of stone and give you an obedient heart. I will put my spirit in you and will see to it that you follow my laws and keep all the commands I have given you. Then you will live in the land I gave your ancestors. You will be My people, and I will be your God* (Ezekiel 36:23-28 GNT).

> *Those who will rebuild you are coming soon, and those who destroyed you will leave. Look around and see what is happening! Your people are assembling—they are coming home! As surely as I am the living God, you will be proud of your people, as proud as a bride is of her jewels. Your country was ruined and desolate—but now it will be too small for those who are coming to live there. And those who left you in ruins will be far removed from you. Your people who were born in exile will one day say to you, "This land is too small—we need more room to live in!" Then you will say to yourself, "Who bore all these children for me? I lost my children and could have no more. I was exiled and driven away—who brought these children up? I was left all alone—where did these children come from?"* (Isaiah 49:17-21 GNT)

> *I, the LORD, say that the time is coming when I will fill the land of Israel and Judah with people and animals. And just as I took care to uproot, to pull down, to overthrow, to destroy, and to demolish them, so I will take care to plant them and to build them up* (Jeremiah 31:27-28 GNT).

The Sovereign LORD says, "When I make you clean from all your sins, I will let you live in your cities again and let you rebuild the ruins. Everyone who used to walk by your fields saw how overgrown and wild they were, but I will let you farm them again. Everyone will talk about how this land, which was once a wilderness, has become like the Garden of Eden, and how the cities which were town down, looted, and left in ruins, are now inhabited and fortified (Ezekiel 36:33-35 GNT).

Then tell them that I, the Sovereign LORD, am going to take all My people out of the nations where they have gone, gather them together, and bring them back to their own land. I will unite them into one nation in the land, on the mountains of Israel. They will have one king to rule over them, and they will no longer be divided into two nations or split into two kingdoms (Ezekiel 37:21-22 GNT).

WORLDWIDE OUTPOURING OF THE HOLY SPIRIT

"Then after I have poured out my rains again, I will pour out my Spirit upon all people. Your sons and daughters will prophesy. Your old men will dream dreams. Your young men will see visions. In those days, I will pour out my Spirit even on servants, men and women alike (Joel 2:28-29).

Immediately following the restoration of Israel as previously detailed, God will then pour out copiously of His Spirit upon all flesh causing the greatest-ever spiritual harvest. The harvest will be reaped by the One New Man comprised of Jewish Messianic believers and Gentile believers many of whom will come to faith in Yeshua from all false religions and particularly from Islam, because God has a special affinity for the seed of Abraham through Ishmael as well as through Isaac.

At the end of this age, which is this present time, there will be a fulfillment of Zechariah 12. Israel will be attacked by all her near neighbors, but Jehovah and the Angel of the Lord will intervene through a miraculous deliverance. Immediately following this astounding victory,

God will pour His Spirit of grace, intercessions, and repentance upon the house of David and the inhabitants of Jerusalem. In the aftermath of this battle when Israel looks around to see where their deliverance came from, they will look upon their Messiah who once was pierced. The nation of Israel will be transformed and enter a period of peace and prosperity that will last until the Gog and Magog war. The Tribulation Messianic Israel, symbolized by the 144,000, together with the innumerable company, will effectively witness to all the nations on earth.

ENDNOTE

1. Yasha (H3467) *Strong's Bible Dictionary.*

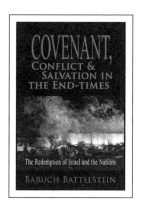

Another exciting title from
DESTINY IMAGE™ EUROPE

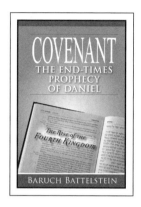

COVENANT
THE END-TIMES PROPHECY OF DANIEL
The Rise of the Fourth Kingdom

by *Baruch Battelstein*

The pages within this book unveil much detail regarding world events, some of which have already occurred, others of which have been in the making for years and are about to happen. Spiritual discernment and understanding of these world events and how they are being woven together by the hand of G-d are essential in order to give one a clear view of the larger picture regarding the rise and the destruction of this fourth kingdom.

Before the Messiah Himself comes to destroy this fourth kingdom and its evil leader, G-d will, in His sovereignty, use it to fulfill His purposes of judgment, both upon the nations and upon His chosen people, the Jews. The connections between the written word of the Lord G-d and the documented course of events taking place in the world today revealed within this book will not leave any doubt of the intentions of G-d's heart—the redemption of His people.

ISBN: 978-88-89127-46-9

Order now from Destiny Image Europe
Telephone: +39 085 4716623 - Fax: +39 085 9431270
E-mail: orders@eurodestinyimage.com

Internet: www.eurodestinyimage.com

Additional copies of this book and other book titles from DESTINY IMAGE™ EUROPE are available at your local bookstore.

We are adding new titles every month!

To view our complete catalog online, visit us at:
www.eurodestinyimage.com

Send a request for a catalog to:

Via Acquacorrente, 6
65123 - Pescara - ITALY
Tel. +39 085 4716623 - Fax +39 085 9431270

"Changing the world, one book at a time."

Are you an author?

Do you have a "today" God-given message?

CONTACT US

We will be happy to review your manuscript for the possibility of publication:

publisher@eurodestinyimage.com
http://www.eurodestinyimage.com/pages/AuthorsAppForm.htm